Praise for *Holding Fire*

"In this beautifully observed book, Bryce Andrews takes us on a courageous and necessary journey toward reconciliation that is as visceral as it is transcendent. The West and its varied inhabitants come alive with every shining line, and when I was done, I found myself wishing for the world that Andrews and his family are daily working toward. This jewel of a book belongs on the shelf with our best Western writers—Norman Maclean, Pam Houston, and Annie Proulx."

—John Vaillant, bestselling author of *The Tiger* and *Fire Weather*

"Very appealing. . . . [Andrews] can write beautifully. . . . Andrews describes the weapon, a Smith & Wesson revolver, almost lovingly. Its craftsmanship, intricate reliability and directness of purpose engaged his artistic sense."

—*Washington Post*

"A gorgeous, lyrical, and moving exploration of the violent legacy that hangs over the West like the inverted fug of a paper mill, woven through with memoir and the surprising journey of the pistol that once belonged to his grandfather. . . . [Andrews] treads a knife edge of vulnerability and scouring grit."

—*Orion*

"A powerful meditation on a rural life of hunting in a world of guns—some of them used for sinister purposes. . . . A welcome, eminently sensible contribution to the literature of the American West—and responsible gun ownership."

—*Kirkus Reviews*

T0035279

"Rancher and conservationist Andrews (*Down from the Mountain*) portrays the transformative beauty and violence of the American West in this evocative outing. . . . It's a bittersweet meditation on the true meaning of the Wild West."

—*Publishers Weekly*

"Regardless of one's stance on guns, Andrews offers insightful reflections on their role in the history of the West."

—*Booklist*

"Bryce Andrews's vibrant, candid account of working as a cowboy in Montana provides a moving meditation on the fragility of life and inevitability of death. . . . As Andrews ruminates on his personal history, he dots his musings with descriptive, emotive prose. *Holding Fire* is a meditation on the past, present, and future of not only Andrews's own life but also the lives of all mortal creatures."

—*BookPage*

"Andrews's heartfelt reflection on the American West confronts one of the region's essential paradoxes: that a place defined by innovation and beauty also has a legacy of horrible violence. For the author, the catalyst is inheriting his grandfather's Smith & Wesson handgun, which carries its own awful history. From his ranch in Montana, Andrews turns to neighbors and family as he seeks a new way to live in the West."

—*Alta*

"An astonishing call to attention. Bryce Andrews's story corrals despair and offers understanding, douses anxiety, and offers wonder. This isn't mere memoir, *Holding Fire* is a song to the West, a talisman of ferocious beauty for a world on edge. Compelling and compassionate, a must-read for all who seek peace in uncertain times."

—Debra Magpie Earling, award-winning author of *Perma Red* and *The Lost Journals of Sacajewea*

"*Holding Fire* is an exquisite meditation on the West and its exemplar, the gun. In poignant and masterful prose, Andrews reflects on his own place and reimagines an instrument better suited, practically and spiritually, to Western lands and cultures, and himself."

—Betsy Gaines Quammen, author of *American Zion*

"Bryce Andrews writes gorgeously of what lies underneath the idealized glamour of the American West. In a voice that is honest and humorous and introspective, he explodes the fetishization of the rugged individual and interrogates the hard realities of what Western gun culture boils down to: killing, with guns designed to bring food and mercy, and guns designed for killing people. How do we live together in this landscape knowing the horrible things we've done to others, and to each other? That is only one of the many questions Andrews asks himself in *Holding Fire*, and we are fortunate to experience his struggle to find answers."

—Chris La Tray, author of *One-Sentence Journal*

HOLDING FIRE

ALSO BY BRYCE ANDREWS

Down from the Mountain

Badluck Way

HOLDING
FIRE

*A Reckoning with the
American West*

BRYCE ANDREWS

MARINER BOOKS

NEW YORK BOSTON

Photographs on pages xvi, 10, 20, 44, 66, 90, 108, 134, 158, 222, and 236 appear courtesy of Colleen Chartier.

Photographs on pages 182, 200, 205, 208, 213, 215, and 218 appear courtesy of Gillian Thornton Andrews.

"Unchopping a Tree" from *The Miner's Pale Children* by W. S. Merwin. Copyright © 2007, 2014 by W. S. Merwin, used by permission of The Wylie Agency LLC.

HarperCollins books may be purchased for educational, business, or sales promotional use. For information, please email the Special Markets Department at SPsales@harpercollins.com.

A hardcover edition of the book was published in 2023 by Mariner Books.

FIRST MARINER BOOKS PAPERBACK EDITION PUBLISHED 2024.

Designed by Chloe Foster

Library of Congress Cataloging-in-Publication Data

Names: Andrews, Bryce, author.
Title: Holding fire : a reckoning with the American West / Bryce Andrews.
Other titles: Reckoning with the American West
Description: First edition. | New York : Mariner Books, [2023]
Identifiers: LCCN 2022045117 (print) | LCCN 2022045118 (ebook) | ISBN 9780358468271 (hardcover) | ISBN 9780063316515 (paperback) | ISBN 9780358466291 (ebook)
Subjects: LCSH: Andrews, Bryce. | Ranchers—Montana—Biography. | Ranch life—Montana. | Montana—Biography. | Hunting—Montana.
Classification: LCC F735.2.A53 A3 2023 (print) | LCC F735.2.A53 (ebook) | DDC 978.6092 [B]—dc23/eng/20220920
LC record available at https://lccn.loc.gov/2022045117
LC ebook record available at https://lccn.loc.gov/2022045118

ISBN 978-0-06-331651-5

23 24 25 26 27 LBC 5 4 3 2 1

For Thea

Finally the moment arrives when the last sustaining piece is removed and the tree stands again on its own. It is as though its weight for a moment stood on your heart.

You listen for a thud of settlement, a warning creak deep in the intricate joinery. You cannot believe it will hold. How like something dreamed it is, standing there all by itself. How long will it stand there now?

The first breeze that touches its dead leaves all seems to flow into your mouth. You are afraid the motion of the clouds will be enough to push it over. What more can you do? What more can you do?

—W. S. MERWIN, "UNCHOPPING A TREE"

Contents

Author's Note

MONTANA IS FULL OF ruins. From where I sit now, I can see a cabin collapsing inward, a barn listing like a holed ship, and the last three upright poles of what was once a long hayshed. Craftspeople built these things with hard work and simple tools. Now the builders are gone and the structures are going. It is humbling to consider.

More humbling still, since those slumping buildings are not really very old. They record just a single late chapter of this region's deep and complicated history, memorializing only a handful of the countless generations that called this place home.

This note reminds the reader that Native people have lived for millennia in what we now call the West. Despite recent centuries of injustice, Indigenous communities still thrive here. The book you hold is set in western and central Montana, in the ancestral territories of the Séliš, Q̓lispé, and Ksanka peoples—Salish, Kalispel, and Kootenai in English translation. It is jarring and necessary to compare those ancestral homelands with the tribes' current reservations.

Consider the Salish and Kootenai tribes on whose reservation, the Flathead, the book's latter half unfolds. From time immemorial, Salish-speaking bands hunted, fished, and traveled across twenty-two million acres of western Montana. The Kootenai people lived to the north, in a territory reaching from Montana into Canada, Idaho, and Washington. The Flathead Indian Reservation, a greatly reduced portion of the tribes' homelands, today totals 1.3 million acres. The geographical math is unmistakably cruel and the violence done to Native cultures extends far beyond loss of land. That hard truth is the context of every Western story. It is worth remembering as you read.

Arlee, Montana
August 2022

HOLDING FIRE

1

DOUBLE EXPOSURE

WE LEFT THE TRUCK and walked through bunchgrass, the whole prairie rattling with August heat. "A bad year for hoppers," Pat Zentz said. Bending down, I cupped one in my hand to feel its kicking. I was eleven years old and looked closely at everything. The insect was heavy for its size and strong.

My father went ahead toward the prairie dog town with a rifle slung from his shoulder, white shirt and cowboy hat stark against late-summer pasture. I had never seen him with a gun before and he carried it well. It was easy to forget that we were visitors on the Zentz Ranch, fresh off the highway from Seattle.

From where he and Pat stopped, I could see the colony sprawling for acres across a plain. Much of the ground was bare, the dirt piled in low pale mounds. The remaining stubble was chewed short, as if the earth had a five-o'clock shadow.

Prairie dogs moved everywhere through the panorama, sunning beside holes, scratching in dust, and standing upright like sentries. A nearer one vanished as if by sleight of hand. Until recently, Pat was telling Dad, there had been enough ferrets, coyotes, foxes, and snakes to keep the population down. Now the dog towns spread farther across his pastures each year, eating grass that livestock needed, digging holes in which cows snapped their legs. Neighbors tried all sorts of things. Poison and floods of irrigation water. Truck exhaust pumped into burrows. Pat spoke quietly now that we stood near the town's edge.

A .22 rifle makes a crisp noise, like the *crack* of a ruler on a desk. Its report is tame compared to bigger guns, but it still rips the fabric of the day. I jumped when my father pulled the trigger. Prairie dogs stood on their hind legs, chittering, peering around.

It was my first experience of the spell of gunfire. My father crooked his finger and a bullet cut the air. Every creature in earshot must have perceived the sound's potency. Dust rose from one of the burrows, spread, and vanished.

"Low," Pat said. "He went down, but you didn't hit him. Shoot at the bottom of your breath. Let it out, then squeeze the trigger."

Dad held the gun to his shoulder, looking through the scope. When the rifle cracked again, the bullet's whistle ended with a *whack*. No dirt plume rose.

Then both of them were firing. Pat's son, Keenan, too. The fusillade drove the remaining dogs to the edges of their burrows, where some stood upright and others tensed on all fours.

When it was done, we entered the colony like heroes in a Western, passing deserted mounds and stripped grassland, hearing nothing but the crunch of our boots. At a shield-shaped burrow, Pat waved me over. A prairie dog lay flat on the dirt. I might have mistaken death for sleep had it not been for a bright strand of viscera. The bullet had cut low through the animal's belly, dragging several inches of intestine through the exit wound.

Fascinated, I bent low.

"Don't touch it," he said. "The fleas carry plague. But I want you to see how *this*"—he held up the rifle—"does *that*." He pointed the barrel at the guts in the dirt.

At the truck, Pat pulled an empty Bud Light from behind the driver's seat. Walking out in the grass, he balanced the can atop a mound.

The single-shot .22 he handed me had been in the Zentz family long enough that both Pat and Keenan had learned to shoot with it. The wooden stock was dark and scarred. The barrel, though oiled, was pitted with rust. It felt good to hold, like a well-used hammer.

Pat showed me how to crack the action and check for a cartridge. I practiced several times before receiving a single round. Slipping the safety off, I set my finger on the trigger.

The details of that afternoon—the weapon's heft and feel, the smells of powder and oiled steel, the metal clicking on metal, the pride of being a boy out shooting with the men—are haloed with a sense of initiation in my memory.

I cannot recall my mother being present. There's irony in that because people almost always remember Colleen Chartier-Andrews. She is taller than most women, striking and thin. Her hair, once very dark brown, has thickened with age into a salt-and-pepper pyramid that passes her shoulders. When I was a child, she wore lace-up combat boots and men's jackets with great style, facing the world with a blue-eyed attention so open and acute that some people fled it. She is a photographer, forever gripped by the artist's urge to collect objects: perfectly round boulders, tree trunks shaped like torsos, the biggest tumbleweed in eastern Washington. So far as I can tell, she believes the world to be full of overlooked fragments of beauty and truth. She hunts these with the ever-present camera of her vocation. Once, she charmed several construction workers into giving her a set of enormous signs from a defunct truck maintenance shop. We ate under ALIGNMENT and gave away LUBRICATION. We took meals in the kitchen, never the dining room. That table was full. The tumbleweed was there.

Mom was with us that day on the Zentz Ranch. It's only because of an image she captured—a lucky, ghostly double exposure on the cheap Holga she favored for her artwork—that I can return to the first time I looked through gunsights and pulled a trigger. She used that image in a gallery show and afterward hung it in our front hallway. The photograph was important to her.

"You were learning something right at the moment when I pressed the shutter," she said once. "Part of your youth was disappearing."

She told me that the lesson had seemed necessary, that she had understood the power of what I was being shown.

"But I was afraid, too. You're ten or eleven. I see arms touching firearms, skin and metal, the sun."

Certain things on this earth belong together and transform each other when they meet. A dust mote meets vapor and rain begins to fall. The drop strikes steel and rust blooms like a flower. Such transformations are hard to reverse. That's how it was for me with the Zentz place, ranching, and Montana. I saw danger and freedom, life and death, wildness and purpose, spread like a feast across the prairie. In the vastness of the land and sky, I recognized the other half of my heart. My mother saw this clearly. She knew that I was started on a road but not how far I would go.

Returning to the ranch each summer, first with my parents and later without them, I learned the rudiments of agricultural work. One evening—I must have been fifteen by then—I came in from a sunburned day afield, ate dinner with the Zentz family, and headed out to hunt prairie dogs in a strong evening wind.

Beyond the backyard, the silos, the rowed shelterbelt trees, and the caraganas, all creation opened. Far in the west, thunderheads had gathered above the Crazy Mountains. The nearer sky was striped with mare's-tail clouds.

The wind gains unexpected power there, unhindered by mountains or trees. It becomes a steady, pressing force, like a river. Power lines wail, eaves howl, buildings shudder and moan. All built things cry in the grip of a prairie wind, but grass revels. It rolls and dances, hissing *yes*, stirring like the fur of a beast.

I walked a half-mile half circle, first upwind with my baseball cap jammed low, then across toward the prairie dog town. The wind made many inextricable sounds. It was the noise of everything being touched. It was hollow. When I crept to the brink of a cutbank, lay down, and loaded the rifle, the day's heat remained in the soil.

I could see across the Duck Creek coulee to where the land canted toward the Yellowstone River. Gusts ran out of that distance, raising dust when they reached the moonscape of the town.

Since my first summer plinking beer cans, I had become a fair shot and a veteran of the prairie dog war. I settled the crosshairs on an upright creature thirty yards away. It flicked its tail three times. I killed it. Hurrying to chamber another round, I expected to see the colony take cover. I was surprised to find the dogs unperturbed, watching the sky for hawks and the horizon for coyotes.

I shot another. Another. They took little notice of the dust that flew when I missed or of neighbors dropping dead. It brought to mind stories I had read about buffalo hunters in the frontier West—men who wore out rifle barrels shooting into herds that did not understand gunfire. After a short while, I realized that the dogs couldn't hear the rifle's noise above the wind. This did not seem unsporting, only lucky.

I made the most of good fortune, firing and reloading for ten minutes while wind tousled the grass. I recall no messiness, physical or moral. The shots looked clean. Animals slid backward into holes or crumpled motionless on the ground. I had learned to kill by watching and practicing, just as I had learned to stretch barbwire. I tried to do it well.

I might have continued until the shells were gone, but the wind slackened when the sun touched the horizon. Pulling the trigger, I let the rifle crack sharp and loud across a moment's relative calm.

With the wind gone, the spell was broken. The remaining dogs scattered and vanished. I could see the sky's blue deepening to transparency in the east, showing the first stars.

Walking through the town, I toed dead prairie dogs into holes. Their limpness stung me. I stood motionless after nudging the last one out of sight, feeling suddenly disgusted.

I hiked sunward through rolling grass, up the diminishing wind toward a section of rimrock where the ground fell away in bands of limestone. Hundreds of feet below, Duck Creek oxbowed through the coulee's wide bottom.

I sat on a flat-topped rock with the rifle across my lap, watching a far-off storm drag scrims of rain. Thunderheads, small in the distance, popped with lightning.

At home, I was the kind of kid who attended to animals. I studied eagles until they drifted out of sight and stayed up late to watch the neighborhood opossum steal cat food. I answered crows. When I found one of those smart black birds on its back, feet jutting up, I mourned it.

This is different, I told myself. *This, with the dogs, is necessary.* Like riding, roping, or fixing engines, it was a skill I'd need to master if I wanted to come to Montana and stay.

Nights in Seattle, I fell asleep rehearsing the steps of saddling a horse, recalling each piece of tack—cinch, latigo, breast collar, martingale—to proof myself against forgetting. I studied the names of prairie grasses, knowing instinctively that I had only a fingertip on my Western dream and would have to keep hold of it.

A red-tail hawk hung cruciform and motionless above the coulee. *Hawks kill them, too,* I thought, *to make a living.*

The last light struck the prairie. Cattle watered on the creek below. Feeling the day's labor as a good aching yoke across my shoulders, I leaned back to better see the sky, keeping my free hand across the rifle. I fixed that moment in my mind and carried it home to the rainy city. I kept it like a secret, remembering how I sat while the sunset burned out. How with one palm on warm stone and the other on barrel steel, I looked across the open country.

You must understand how badly I wanted to be a cowboy. After I visited the ranch, I believed with a child's certainty that I had found my true and proper home. It was not only the place that caught me, but also its people—Pat, Suzie, and their three boys. Whether the problem was a stalled tractor or a rattlesnake in the yard, the Zentz family knew what to do. They got on with things— tinkered until the engine came to life, spliced rusty wire, shot the head from the snake—and laughed everything off around the dinner table. The boys had a feral quality that I admired. They drove unlicensed on the county roads and owned horses, living prince-like in a hardscrabble kingdom. People were not that way where I was from.

Once I saw it all, I could not stop dreaming. In quiet moments all through childhood, I entertained a Western fantasy in which the sky's broad dome appeared first, its sun a magnet tugging upward on my heart. Beneath that sky were toothlike distant mountains, whole island ranges scattered on a plain like toys. In the tawny middle distance were many scattered cattle.

Nearer was a horseman on a promontory from which the land's sweep could be seen. He wore a wide-brimmed hat, blue jeans, old boots. He was proud, straight-backed, and alert. Mount and rider stood motionless, looking across the pan-orama, unmistakably at home. At times, I thought I might grow up to become that man. On other nights, I despaired of ever being so proud.

There were always firearms in the dream. I remember that clearly. A lever-action rifle in the man's saddle scabbard or a revolver on his hip. The guns might have been single-action or double, made by Smith & Wesson or Colt; but despite this variance, they were recognizable as the ones packed by everyone from Earp to Eastwood, the ones Charlie Russell painted into the hands of buckaroos and cavalry soldiers. They were the guns that won the West.

The actual weapons are heavier than most people imagine and more beautiful. They glint and shine: refined machines with trigger, sear, springs, and hammer arranged in hidden synchronicity; marvels of engineering that fit the human hand better than a glove. In many of the stories I heard when I was young, such guns were magic wands, instruments of justice, and protection against the wilderness. They were blued-steel links to our heroic past.

2

HOW IT CAME TO ME

MY FATHER TAUGHT ME to do no harm. A lifelong man of peace and a conscientious objector to the Vietnam War, he was also the one to deliver the gun—a Smith & Wesson revolver that had belonged to my grandfather—into my hands.

On the day he brought it to me, we both got up early. He drove out through tidy neighborhoods, threading a path through Seattle's gridlock, beginning the eight-hour trip to Montana. I woke up on the cattle ranch I managed near the town of Deer Lodge, walked through a dirt yard, and let myself into the corrals. The sky was black. Horses ran circles in the round pen, bucking as if unmannered by the bone-colored moon.

I meant to catch my favorite gelding, a lanky bay with a blaze that widened down the line of his nose. He had no breeding, but he had hard hooves and a tremendous heart. In the years I worked ranches, I never met a horse that could travel with him. By now that gelding is reduced to bones and a patch of greener grass somewhere, but that morning he was all speed and muscle, a dark horse in his prime, loping. I caught and saddled him, and we rode out on a cattle trail with the dog trotting behind, cresting a long ridge as the eastern sky blued and fired.

The Sapphires, a range of round-topped, half-timbered mountains, look smooth and unformidable from a distance—like eggs in an open carton. Up close, they are rough country, with tangled dead-end logging roads and miles-long stands of doghair pine.

I rode for an hour up Orofino Mountain, then started downhill on a zigzag course, picking up bands of scattered cattle. A dozen pairs became twenty, twenty became fifty, and fifty a river of heavy-walking beasts following a rutted road south. The herd had its own momentum so I could detour to roust lingerers from the shadowed places that livestock favor in late summer.

In one such spot, I urged my horse between a pair of close-set trees. It was tight, but I pressed my luck in pursuit of a calf. As we slipped between the trunks, I felt a thick broken branch—a stob, my neighbors would have called it—wedge into my stirrup. It happened fast, and my stirrup twisted backward as the horse moved ahead. He took another step and the stirrup brought him up short.

No horse likes being caught that way. Shying, he threw his weight against leather and the sinews of my leg. He pulled until my eyes shut from pain and the saddle shifted to one side.

He will buck and tear my foot off, I thought.

The animal shook with strain and panic. It was like an earthquake's foreshock and I knew enough to be afraid. I've had metal plates and screws in my arm since I was twenty, a small monument to the danger of spooked horses.

When the branch snapped, the horse took two leaps forward. We stood still—saddle akimbo, both trembling. My ankle ached, but it took weight when I climbed to the ground. There was a short scrape beading blood across the gelding's ribs. The branch, broken flush with the trunk, looked like all the others in the forest.

By midmorning, I rode behind not less than two hundred pairs, the animals raising dust in which I wallowed. Shortly after midday, I came to a good place on Cottonwood Mountain and turned the herd from the road into thigh-high fescue.

I settled the cattle there. As mothers found their bawling calves, it grew quiet enough for me to hear the sound of general vigorous chewing. Sitting the horse in peace, I looked across my dirty, beautiful, chosen life and felt equal to it.

The feeling was rare. Before that summer, even as my seasonal ranch jobs stretched into years of work, I felt like I was riding a train without a ticket and would someday be thrown off. *What right had a young man born and raised in the wet heart of Seattle*, I asked myself, *to saddle horses under Montana's endless sky?*

I kept working and no reckoning came. I became manager of the Dry Cottonwood Creek Ranch, shouldering responsibility for the lives of 130 cows, five bulls, and all their Red Angus get. I bought and sold horses, stretched barbwire, and loaded fall calves into cattle trailers. Twice already, I had watched those potbellied semis clatter away, turned to face a pen full of bawling mothers, and started over.

I built a house for myself, framing a one-bedroom living space into the southeast corner of a sheet-metal barn. The barndominium, I called it.

What I had on Dry Cottonwood—responsibility, solitude, and challenging work—convinced me at last that I had come into the West to stay. My contract had no end date. The job was mine until I wore out or failed, and I was determined not to fail.

LATER IN THE DAY, descending from the mountains toward the barn, I caught the glint of sun on a car in the yard and knew my father had arrived. There is something different about cars from the city. Even when dirty, city cars shine.

Something like that is true of people. At thirty-nine years old, I have now lived here long enough to weather. I look different from my childhood friends who remained in Seattle. Not older but harder used. Crow's feet mark my eyes and scars adorn my knuckles. Recently, I've noted the development of stringy, corded muscle in my arms, neck, and shoulders—not youth's smooth swollen strength but something less pretty and more durable. Sometimes I think that I am starting to look like a ranch truck, dinged and scraped, marked and sustained by use. I take pride in this. It also worries me because I know what happens to those trucks in the end.

As I crossed Dry Cottonwood and climbed from its channel, my father rounded the barn's far corner into the light of a low sun. He wore his traveling-through-Montana uniform of a fisherman's shirt and shorts, and waved when he saw me.

Closing the distance, we scrutinized each other as parents and children do when they have been separated. His legs were spindly. That this should be my first impression seemed ungenerous.

Perhaps I was harsh because I take after him. My legs are quite like his. We have the same complexion, which sun and wine redden as if they were drawing blood to the surface. We have dark hair and a similar manner of walking, so people know from a distance who we are to each other.

In the eyes of such strangers, we would have been a pair of lanky related men. Walking out from the barn: a tall and broad-chested father in his early sixties, black eyebrows like gull wings, a high forehead, and a straight nose that was neither beak nor button. Coming in from the fields: his son of twenty-eight, the father's shape remade with a bit less flesh and a set of flaring ears.

My parents seldom arrived on the ranch without gifts. Where generosity was concerned, they were relentless saints. Season by season, they filled the barndominium with comforts.

I came to have a rocking chair from Crate & Barrel, IKEA shelving, and good cookware. I finished out the place's bathroom by installing a toilet rumored to have once belonged to Bill Gates that was scavenged by a contractor friend of my mother's and hauled to Deer Lodge in a Subaru.

My parents gave me smoked salmon and dark chocolate. Convinced that a hard life should include a few soft things, my mother always brought pillows. After she had been at it for a few years, I counted more than thirty, including throws.

Their gifts tended to almost, but not quite, suit the circumstances of my life. Since the gear required by a ranching life could not be found in Seattle's shops, it was rare for my parents to bring something I could truly use. Rarer still was for me to hunger after a particular object and anticipate its coming. My father understood this. He was not long in walking to the back of his car, rummaging among fishing tackle and duffel bags, and opening the lid of a plastic cooler.

Setting aside bread and other staples, he rolled back a dish towel and retrieved a triangular cloth case from where the ice packs should have been. The way he did it made me expect something illicit, like state secrets or a brick of weed.

"I didn't know the rules about crossing state lines," he said.

When I slid the revolver free, it gleamed blackly in the late sun. I held the weapon across both palms, long barrel pointing toward the mountains. Looking at the gun, my father said: "As a thing, it's kind of beautiful."

The compliment was unlikely from a man who had refused to be a soldier. It was to be expected, perhaps, from the director of a contemporary art museum—the job my father held for much of his professional life.

The gun was finely made. Every inch of it, from the checkered grip to the bore's machined perfection, proclaimed the skill of master craftspeople. It had a precise balance, evident as I picked it up; and when I pressed the catch above the trigger, the cylinder swung out with a noise like a watch marking seconds. Six empty chambers yawned up, each hungry for its bullet. I snapped the cylinder shut. He was right, the gun was beautiful.

"Your grandfather would have liked it coming out here," he said. "Where it can be useful."

This was after my father's father, Robert Thorne Andrews, lost his strength and some of his faculties, and had to move to the kind of nursing home where nobody owns a gun. Another year would pass before my grandfather died, but death was around us. It was in the tidy room my father visited twice a week. I sometimes joined those visits on the phone but not as often as I might have. I never knew what to say. Privately, I saw my father's unvarying attendance and care as a lavish, possibly excessive, gift. The two men were not close in the way some fathers and sons become. In the way my father and I are, for example.

My grandfather contained a vein of remoteness. He was not cold, mean, or unaccountable, but neither did he ask questions or unburden himself to us. Because of this, I found it hard to remember much about him even before he passed away. He fought in the Second World War and afterward worked for a long time at Sears, in home furnishings. He liked fishing and wore the type of thin plaid button-up shirts that older men favor in rural Montana. Much more than that, I could not say. To carry away so little left me with a sense of having wronged him.

My father held out a full cartridge belt, the leather stiff from lack of use. If the gun had been well-kept, the belt looked forgotten. It stunk of closets and oxidation. Mildew whitened the holster. Corroded by the salt air of western Washington, the shell casings had wept blue trails across the loops that held them.

As we ate on the porch, I kept expecting my father to say more about the gun. I waited for a story, but he volunteered nothing. Cold bottles sweating in our hands, we watched the sun dip past the westward mountains.

After a while, I asked why his father had bought the revolver and what he had used it for.

"I don't know. Protection? Or target shooting, but I don't remember him doing much of it. After what he saw in Europe, I'd have thought he'd want to be as far from weapons as possible.

"He did a lot of things I don't understand. I'm sure of this, though—he wanted you to have the gun. He admired your life. Liked hearing stories about it. I think he could have been happy out here."

After my father went in to bed, I stayed on the porch examining the revolver in the soft light from my windows. The weapon smelled of oil and my fingers left prints on the bluing. Its wooden grip was warm to the touch, the metal colder than night air. I examined it closely, touching characters stamped into the barrel.

On one side: SMITH & WESSON.

On the other: .357 MAGNUM.

My grandfather's gun. *He carried and shot it,* I thought, *and now it has come to me.* Sitting in the dark, I felt a new responsibility. His gun was in my care. Someday I would hand it on. That inheritance and legacy matched the kind of man I had become.

I aimed the revolver at the night, feeling its weight as I stretched out my arm. I tried this first with my left, dominant hand, then with my right—the one crushed years ago by a horse. The wooden grip was sized precisely for a palm like mine.

East of where we live now, past several mountain ranges, is a valley big enough to bend horizons like the ocean does. Anglers in the Andrews family have gone there for three generations. My grandfather came first, but it was my father who made fishing the Madison River into an art form in our family. He was the one who recognized Three Dollar Bridge as a pocket-water Promised Land, who found the West Fork campsite, who learned to wait out midday heat by swimming in Cliff Lake, who tied flies all winter at our kitchen table in Seattle. I wouldn't be surprised to learn that he crafted each nymph, dry, and streamer with a specific hole or riffle in mind. He was that sort of fisherman. My father put leader to water in almost every river and stream in southwest Montana, but he loved the Madison best.

All three of us cherished the place, but I was the only one to live there. Long before my father put the Smith & Wesson in my hands, when I was just out of college, I moved to the Madison to work on the Sun Ranch.

I wish you could see the valley as it was then: huge and pinnacle-edged, swept clean by wind, with distant herds and few structures of any kind. Rolling south on the two-lane highway, grasslands stretching off to either side, I seemed to enter a vestige of the world before the fall. I wish we could climb into the truck and go back there, but the place has changed. It remains beautiful, but there are too many new houses.

The Madison's eastward peaks—Sphinx, Helmet, and others—are fine to behold, but the valley's beating heart is sunlight. Late on a summer afternoon, it floods across the Gravelly Range. Clear, stark, and yellow, the light singles things out from the landscape, showing each in turn.

See this lone juniper on a slope of August fescue. Pruned five feet up by browsing cattle, it is a green-black gumdrop on a pin. See, says that remarkable light, how a tree contains uncommon darkness.

Look at these antelope crossing the plain, hides afire. One hundred white-flanked pronghorn, small on the expanse, stick-legged. See them run, eddying together, beading into a long thin line, disappearing into cottonwood galleries along a creek. What scent or creature, the light bids you ask, made those antelope run?

3

LOVING RIFLES

EVEN THE MILLIONAIRES WHO owned neighboring spreads had to admit that the Sun Ranch is the jewel of the Madison. It has the right combination of expanse and relief, the loveliest balance of timber with grass, a front-row seat to gorgeous mountains. The Sun had eighteen thousand such acres and something more, an ineffable quality that compelled and seduced people.

Everyone from West Yellowstone to the town of Ennis knew the Sun, and most people coveted it one way or another. They wanted to hunt the meadows, hike the foothills, look for shed antlers, visit the semi-secret hot spring, or drop by the local cowboy-and-fisherman bars to gossip about how many elk, how many wolves, and what mistakes the owner was making.

It's hard to get people to agree on anything about such a place, but of this much everyone was certain: Among the Madison's several dozen large ranches, that thirty-mile receiving line of windswept, haughty beauties, the Sun reigned queen.

It sits at the high end of the valley. Behind its uppermost fence is granite-tipped wilderness, and beyond that wilderness is Yellowstone National Park. Something issues from the peaks, pouring down like the snowmelt does in spring, anointing the Sun with qualities of an older world.

Fresh out of school, I could imagine no better place to live or job to do. I slept in a bunkhouse beside the Madison River and woke to tasks that sent me alone into the foothills. It was my lot to saddle a horse and ride all day without roads. Indeed, I had to do so if I wanted to keep drawing wages. There was no way but horseback to cross the steep, folded drainages where we summered cattle.

I took to the life wholeheartedly with a single exception: Every so often, when I was alone in certain wild places, I got scared. Stretching barbwire in a deep-shadowed thicket or following a stock-water line upcanyon to its source, I'd be gripped by an unexpected terror.

Sometimes there was a reason, like the reek of a bear or the tracks of a mountain lion. More often it was just a feeling of peril that leapt into me from the surrounding stones and trees, standing my hair on end.

I could not keep from seeing death. I felt a lion's breath on the nape of my neck or conjured a grizzly from the undergrowth—a beast with small intent eyes and a pink-gummed yawning mouth—charging so quickly that I didn't have time to turn away.

At such moments, I could hardly breathe or walk. It was an awful panic, one that did not diminish with the passing weeks. The other men who worked on the ranch carried guns in the mountains and never seemed to be afraid.

I envied their impunity but found it hard to relax when anyone had a pistol. Sometimes, when we were out fixing fence, my coworker would bend down to pick up his end of a brace rail and the gun on his hip would point straight at me. He had an open-bottomed holster, so I'd see the barrel staring like an unblinking pupil. I always froze when it happened and never forgot the feeling of looking into a small dark hole that death can fly from at an instant. I can still see the point of aim panning upward as he stooped, rising from my knees to my head. It made me think of shot prairie dogs, their guts strung out and shining. "*This*," I could hear Pat Zentz saying, "does *that*."

We didn't just have pistols. Rifles hung in rear-window racks and saddle scabbards. Shotguns, often loaded with the noise-maker rounds we used to frighten bears and wolves, leaned beside doors. We were seldom without firearms, the weapons following us through workdays like well-trained dogs at heel. None of those guns belonged to me, though. I had moved to Montana unarmed.

Neighbors I met—old-school family ranchers, hunting guides, and hired cowboys—found this strange. Some of them grinned at the idea of a gunless ranch hand. Others took it as an insult. Looking down from her saddle, one silver-haired rancher who pastured cattle on the Sun asked how I could possibly protect her cows. She was wind-burnished, weathered, legit—every rawhide inch a creature of the place and way of life that I admired.

Her judgment was clear and searing, suggesting that by coming unprepared I had revealed myself not only as a poor specimen of cowboy but also less than a complete man.

I often thought about going into Ennis and buying a rifle. I had money saved, since there were few ways to waste it on the Sun, and knew that getting a gun in rural Montana was as easy as walking into the nearest sporting-goods shop and picking one from the racks on the wall.

The fact remained that I was not raised to own weapons. Most of this came from my father. While my mother, the photographer, made sure I understood that beauty hid in the mundane scenes of the world, it was my father who shaped my opinion of violence.

He grew up in Los Angeles in the 1950s before the city had metastasized. The coast was livable then, even beautiful, and he loved Long Beach, where his grandparents kept a house by the Pacific. His mother, Theodora, was peripherally related to the Chandler-Otis clan—a far-West dynasty responsible for founding the *LA Times*, desiccating the Owens Valley to slake the city's thirst, and platting Hollywood.

My father's family tree is meticulously pruned on both sides, giving the impression that we descend from captains of industry, statesmen, warriors, and otherwise world-shaking sires. On this side of the Atlantic, one of its deepest roots is William Bradford, the former governor of Plymouth Colony. After him come soldiers, doctors, businessmen, and bankers, among them an eminent Chicago surgeon whose portrait hung in our house framed with a printed quotation.

> GOOD CHARACTER IS ITS OWN SUFFICIENT DEFENSE. WIN IT, PERFECT IT, AND FEAR NOTHING, FOR CHARACTER IS THE MIGHTIEST THING UNDER GOD IN THE UNIVERSE.—EDMUND ANDREWS, M.D.

Several generations after Edmund comes my grandfather, who fought in Europe and later bought the Smith & Wesson. Then comes my father, who was drawn magnetically toward art instead of commerce, politics, or war. My father, who painted signs for peace marches from LA to Berkeley; who, when the Army called his draft number, refused to shoulder a gun.

His family was not pleased. One summer afternoon in 1971, my father sat in a wicker chair on the porch of his grandparents' house looking over Alamitos Bay, thinking westward across the Pacific's endless miles toward burning Vietnam. Around him was paradise: warm sun, fresh breeze, a patio party, midcentury upper-crust California. Beyond the bay, sunlight set the stucco, clapboard, finned Cadillacs, and palm fronds glowing.

Opposite him, arrayed on deck chairs, sat a half circle of family friends—the men mostly veterans of the Second World War, the women faithful to their men and Nixon—holding forth about the domino theory and the younger generation's failure to answer their nation's call.

After cocktails, they called my father a coward. His aunt cried in the pretty coastal sunshine and asked if he knew how many people had died for his freedom. His father had served. His grandfather, too, and so on up the line of Hammond-Otis-Andrews men. All those generations had furthered and protected the American experiment. Did that, my father's elders asked, mean anything to him at all?

I think so. Fifty years on, he gets anxious when talking about that afternoon. All the same, he did not go to war.

His application for conscientious objector status is a mimeographed relic with a handful of blank lines below each of four neatly typed questions. As clear as a drill sergeant, as neat as a recruit's haircut, the form's layout says: *Keep it short, kid.*

Dad's response was eighteen pages, on which he typed: "Life is sacred for myself and all living things in that we participate totally in each other. I must maintain myself as a creative instrument, harmonious with the greater creative process."

And: "War continues the vicious circle of power—there are those who dominate and those who are dominated. The division between the two sides calls forth hate and bitterness."

And: "I must not resist evil with evil. It is purposeless to answer the sword with the sword."

He quoted Christ, Gandhi, and Dr. Martin Luther King Jr. He was denied, of course. Of course, he appealed.

"You have a sister, don't you?" a man asked him at the draft board hearing. "What would you do if somebody broke into your house to kill her? *Rape* her?"

"If that happened tomorrow," Dad replied, "I'd try to keep my family safe. I'd do whatever I could to stop a killer, but war is different."

Going to war, he told them, meant signing on for violence. It made him the housebreaker rather than a good son defending his family.

Perhaps a quick tongue and eighteen pages of metaphysics were enough to stymie people at the Selective Service System, but there were other factors, too: Dad had been to boarding school and could present himself well to authority. He was white, well-off, and descended from a family that drew water in Southern California. He could have passed for a son of the men questioning him.

For some stew of these reasons, the draft board shunted Dad toward two years of alternative service. He found acceptable work in Seattle—my grandparents having moved north a year before—at what was then called a "home for disturbed boys."

My mother went with him, the pair having met just after Dad's draft number had been called. They built a life in the rainy city. They had a son.

We lived in a safe neighborhood near the heart of Seattle, our street opening toward a park and the gray water of Portage Bay. Water beaded on the rhododendrons. I lacked for nothing but toy weapons, an innocence so pristine that when I first encountered a plastic pistol at a neighbor's house I gripped it sideways and peered through the trigger guard. Holding the gun, I framed a bit of the kitchen in what I thought to be a viewfinder and mimed the pressing of a camera's shutter. My parents both like that story.

One winter evening when I was nine, my grandfather agreed

to show me the rifle and revolver he kept in a back room. With a strange fire in my chest, I followed him down the hallway of his house—a dark, low, sprawling rambler in the rain-fat cedar forest outside Issaquah.

I've wondered why my father didn't object to this. Perhaps, knowing that nobody grows up entirely innocent in America, he believed weapons would enter my life with or without his permission.

First came the lever-action Winchester, with its shining octagonal barrel and satin-finished stock. The rifle had a cattle-drive scene engraved on the receiver and carried no marks of use that I can recall.

Taking the revolver from a high shelf, my grandfather unsnapped the leather holster's keeper. Even unloaded, the six-shooter tugged my hands toward the floor. I had never held anything with such gravity. His rifle didn't scare me, but that Smith & Wesson did. Maybe that's why it fascinated me.

Part of my interest also came down to contrast: In a landscape and childhood where many things were soft, the .357 was uncompromisingly cold and hard. I liked that. Though I never told anyone, something moved in me when I first took the revolver in hand. The weapon was simple and powerful. It was unapologetically, purposefully itself. I had a sense, perhaps only a hope, that I was that way, too.

In the back room, my father and grandfather stood on either side of me, filling my head with warnings. For their differences, both were careful men. They must have been talking caution, but I don't recall a word. The revolver held my attention. It had a dark magnetism, as cliffs, coiled snakes, and nighttime water do. From the start, that .357 had a way of swallowing my gaze. I couldn't look without falling in.

A few months after I arrived in the Madison Valley to work on the Sun, my boss purchased a rifle quite like the one my grandfather had owned. Although the foreman said the new weapon was to be shared among our cattle crew, it seemed intended for me, the only hand without a gun of his own. What we called the "ranch rifle" stayed in my work truck. I kept it oiled. I took it with me when I slept out to guard cattle from wolves.

I was relieved to have the ranch rifle thrust into my hands. It comforted and steadied me. In dark timber, as I stood among the bones of some recently killed ungulate and listened to grizzlies moving through thickets, I would grip the rifle and feel something flow from its steel into my flesh. The change was immediate. I could breathe and walk. I could do my job without the stain of fear.

That ranch .30–30 leaned in a corner of my living room when my dad came to visit in late summer. When he asked about it, I cited bears and wolves, and broken-legged steers that needed killing. The needs and dangers of my work were as real, I said, as the rifle's remedy. He seemed to understand, but he still didn't like to see a gun beside the door.

We were talking after dinner with night against the windows when a pickup raced past my bunkhouse and went up the main ranch road. It was a loud, lifted rig—a Saturday-night truck in pursuit of trouble. Because I was in charge of keeping poachers and other trespassers off the ranch, I stood up from the table, grabbed the rifle, and was headed out when Dad stopped me.

"Better to have it and not need it," I said, parroting a cowboy I knew, "than need it and not have it."

"If you bring that gun," he said, "you might end up using it. If you don't, you won't."

I took the gun. Driving uphill as fast as I could without losing the road, I turned my father's words over in my mind. *I know this place,* I thought. *He doesn't.* Dropping a hand to where the .30–30 was tucked between the passenger seat and center console, I could not put his doubts from my mind.

The ranch was immaculately black, with stars vaulted in a clear sky. Catching up with the truck, I flashed my high beams and watched the trespasser brake in a place too narrow to pull alongside him. I stopped in his dust and looked down at the rifle. I wanted it with me, but in the end, I walked empty-handed up the road to argue with a rough man through a rolled-down window.

He was on private land, I explained to him, and would have to leave. He claimed to have permission to cross the ranch but could not give a name when I asked who he had it from.

I told him again that he couldn't drive farther. In spite of my efforts to keep calm, we moved through the preamble to a fight. He was a big man, perhaps ten years my senior, with a camo hat pulled low. Once or twice, he made a fist—a thick, knurled, workman's fist with skin tugged pale across the knuckles—and struck the door. I understood that he could beat the shit out of me. All I could see of his eyes was a glint angry enough to charge the space between us.

Around that time, a couple of valleys over, a highway patrolman pulled up behind a truck on a similarly lonely stretch of gravel. Everyone who lived around there saw the dashcam video, and nobody who had the job of stopping trespassers on backroads—a task that often falls to ranch hands—forgot it.

In the video, a patrol car pulls up behind a parked three-quarter-ton Ford. The truck's driver—a tall middle-aged white guy—is out quickly, walking toward the cruiser. In his billed cap, faded Carhartt jacket, and Wranglers, he looks like every rancher. After taking a few steps, the man stands straighter, craning at the officer, maybe checking to see who he is. That's not strange on the outskirts of a small town. The man takes a look—less than a second—before turning back toward his truck.

"Come back here," says the patrolman from just outside the frame. He sounds steady and collected, a professional on the job.

The guy doesn't come. He takes another step toward the truck and a shotgun emerges fast—not from a rack but off the seat. The sound of his shots—one, another—register faintly on the dashboard camera. The officer's groan is louder, as is the salvo he returns.

The patrolman misses. The guy reaches into his truck—never hurrying—for shells. He loads the shotgun methodically, efficiently, like he's in a duck blind between flights. The officer shoots another quick, wild burst, causing the man to lean into the cab for shelter. Most of his torso disappears for a few seconds, then he's back firing. The birdshot and wadding show as a faint shadow leaving the barrel.

The whole thing unfolds too calmly. The gunman pops off muffled shots. The officer groans offscreen, a dying man making no more noise than a sleeper shifting position.

That patrolman was twenty-three years old. So was I when I stood in the road with my heart beating through my ribs, the trespasser staring me down, not speaking anymore, just watching with narrowed eyes. The night was still—wind gone, stars brighter every minute, settling dust in my nose—and gravid with violence. The moment waited on me as a cartridge waits for the firing pin to fall.

I craved the rifle's smooth reassurance. I wanted to hold the gun between us, take strength, and send him packing, but the work truck and the rifle were unreachable from where I stood in the road. Lacking any weapon, I talked, repeating many times that we were on private property and he couldn't go on.

We would drive together, I told him with all the force I could muster, ahead to where the road topped a bench. I described the turnings and gates we would pass, and how we would come to a place where willows grew in the ditch. He would see the willows—could not miss them in his headlights. He would notice where the road widened, where we could both turn around. I talked for a long time. He acknowledged nothing, but we seemed to be stepping back from the brink.

I don't recall him agreeing to the plan. Leaving his window, I walked to my own truck and eased it ahead. We drove in a slow, tense convoy up another quarter mile. *He won't turn,* I worried. *Then what will you do?*

At the uppermost end of the wide place with the willows, at the last possible moment, the man swerved and backed. He passed my open window as he started downhill, looking straight ahead, his profile showing dimly in the dash's orange glow.

Following him down the road, my lights slewed across the long gun racked in his rear window, flashing on steel with each turn.

BY FALL OF THAT first year on the Sun, I understood a truth of ranching: For every birth, a death. For every calf romping in June's green fields, a carcass cooling somewhere. I had come to believe that getting by in the world required violence. If I wanted to make my living out here, I decided, I would have to kill to eat.

There were always whitetail deer around the bunkhouse, traveling narrow trails through the brushy corridor of the Madison River. In October, when everyone I knew went looking for meat, I tried my hand at hunting. I bought a doe tag, borrowed a rifle, donned an orange vest over my work jeans and jacket, and crept into the backyard willows at dusk.

Whitetails are seldom at peace. They are hunted by humans,

dogs, coyotes, mountain lions, wolves, and opportunistic bears—
everything medium-bodied or larger with pointed teeth. It is their
great misfortune to be the ideal size, often guileless, and succulent.

The deer live among us in fields and along irrigation canals,
fattening on grain crops and alfalfa. Outside hunting season, they
grow used to the presence of humans. The ones around my bunkhouse heard our trucks every morning and evening, and sometimes grazed beside the corrals while I drank beer on the porch. I
saw the same bucks often enough to know them.

The first time cannot really be called a hunt. I saw a few deer—
three does and a half-grown fawn—through my kitchen window.
Taking up the borrowed rifle, I walked into the thickets beside
the river. The deer trotted, nonplussed, behind a screen of willows.
I saw their shapes through leafless branches, one walking ahead,
dropping her head to eat while the others pushed on. At fifty
yards, I singled out the foremost doe and watched her lead the
group out of sight behind thicker brush.

I stood ready, rifle in hand, watching for the deer to come into
a clear space. At last, one did. I saw its nose, eyes, and active ears.
When the neck showed, I looked through the scope. At such a
modest distance, the animal filled the reticle.

I will admit that I had built the moment up into a rite of passage. In the upper Madison, hunting was something all grown
men seemed to do.

I must do the thing correctly, I thought, as my heart hammered
and the crosshairs settled behind the animal's shoulder. *Shoot well.*
I bent forward, stretching out my neck and straining my right
eye until the world contracted to the scope's small round field of
view. The deer remained broadside, motionless. *Now,* I thought,
slipping off the safety and bringing my finger against the trigger.
It must be now.

I was ready for the noise but not the impact, which was like a punch in the face, that followed on its heels. Recoiling from the pain, I took a blind step backward, hooked my heel on a willow root, and landed spread-eagled in the grass. Clapping a hand to my right eye, I kept up a steady pressure until the throbbing subsided enough for me to think, then I stared at the smeared half circle on my palm. I found the gun in the grass beside me. The scope's metal eyepiece was clean. When something hits that hard and quickly, it can be gone before blood has time to flow.

Nobody has to know about this, I thought, forgetting the half-moon gash on my face. Walking to where the deer had been standing, I found a spot of red on the ground. That part was easier than I had imagined. Fresh blood is bright with vitality. It glistens on fallen leaves.

A blood trail is easy to find but hard to follow, especially when the light is failing and the hunter sheds occasional droplets of his own. I searched in widening circles, then ran home for a flashlight. *Perhaps it was wounded,* I thought grimly, wondering what to do if it crossed the river onto someone else's land. The idea of a doe swimming the ice-cold Madison with a ruined front shoulder or a bullet in her gut made me feel like a son of a bitch. I would look until it was pitch-dark, I decided, and continue in the morning for as long as it took. If at the end I had not found a dead white-tail, I'd punch my tag and be done with my hunting experiment.

Doubling back, I nearly tripped over the carcass. It was closer to the bloody spot than I had expected, twenty yards off in long grass and leaves. The bullet had entered behind the front shoulder, piercing both lungs. My perfect shot had felled a six-month-old fawn.

I knew how it had happened. The herd had passed behind the willows with a doe in the lead, but the incautious fawn had been

the first to emerge, alone, on the other side. Without other animals for scale, half-grown fawns are hard to distinguish from
their mothers. I know the difference now—a doe has a longer face
while a fawn's body is taller in proportion to its length—but that
night I could do nothing but curse my inexperience, gut the small
creature, and carry him home.

I hung, skinned, and butchered the fawn in the machine shop.
The ranch's other hands were kind enough not to rib me about
my pint-size kill. They were less delicate about the fact that I had
been "scoped." All winter, I opened butcher-paper packets of miniature steaks and felt pangs of conscience. Even so, the meat was
excellent. I resolved to try again next autumn, this time for elk in
the high peaks of the Madison Range, and to get the thing right.

THE FOLLOWING OCTOBER, I entered the Madisons just
south of the Sun Ranch. The trail rose from a gravel turnaround,
switchbacking at times as it followed Papoose Creek between
slopes of grass and glacial stones. Once I was in the defile, there
was no noise but running water. Snow was falling, big flakes blur-
ring distant peaks, covering the ground and melting on my pack
and shoulders. Except for the pines, the land was all black rock
and white snow.

I watched for familiar landmarks: the cow skull marking an
uphill turn, the dense forest where wolves had killed cattle a summer ago, the place where the path cut north through folded country toward Moose Creek and the best elk range in the Madisons.

The temperature dropped and I pretended for a while that it
was because I was climbing higher. Within an hour, as the west
wind turned bitter and sweat froze to my skin, I knew winter's
first true storm had arrived.

Toiling beneath a stuffed pack with my newly purchased hunting rifle slung from my shoulder, I took some comfort in the fact that as long as I did nothing foolish like wander in a whiteout it would be hard to get lost. I knew the mountains behind the Sun Ranch as well as anyone, having herded cattle there. The rules were simple: Going uphill took me farther into the wilderness. Coming downhill brought me out again.

I labored into the wild country for a day, camping finally along the north fork of Sun Creek. Darkness came early and lasted an interminable while. That night, in the valley below, a friend of mine measured the temperature at four degrees Fahrenheit. Donning every stitch of clothing I had, I shivered myself warm and finally slept. Waking was an upward swim.

Climbing to a high point through ankle-deep weightless snow, I waited for daylight under all the stars. The morning held an aching clarity, a bottomless montane cold that poured through the neck and cuffs of my jacket, robbing heat from my core. My hunting rifle, a wooden-stocked Ruger .30–06, was a ghost of itself. Overnight, my breath had rimed it with thick frost. *What happened to weapons in such arctic conditions?* I wondered. *Could bullets still fire? At what temperature did gunmetal shatter?*

Curled against a glacial boulder, I waited as dawn turned the east faintly, then promisingly, blue. When the light permitted, I turned my binoculars on the hills and was instantly rewarded. High up on a ridge to the north, several dozen elk grazed a grassy spine toward thick timber. I watched them move along a game trail, calves dallying or skittering ahead, cows pausing to scent the air, all their exhalations pluming and visible at the distance of a half mile.

Stamping life into my feet, I supposed it would be a simple matter to clamber up, keep hidden, and ambush the herd in the trees. *A short hunt*, I thought.

I climbed, slipping often in the immaculate snow. Air ran thin and cold through my lungs. When the sun showed, it felt like warm water poured across my skin.

At the tree line, I entered where the elk had disappeared. It was quiet under the canopy, and I ran the rifle's action slowly, chambering a cartridge and checking the safety.

Hunting such a forest takes patience. The eye has to outpace the body, interrogating the small spaces between branches. Novice that I was, I hurried through the trees, expecting at every moment to overtake the herd. I found nothing but tracks, scat, and the hot scent of freshly departed creatures lingering in the air.

It was enough to draw me on. I climbed higher, always following sign so new that it seemed the elk must have been barely out of sight. By late morning, I had pursued the herd up a huge foothill—a nine-thousand-foot-tall crenelated wedge known locally as the Pyramid. Atop it, forced to a halt by my stomach, I sat on a stone and looked across a panorama of avalanche chutes, headwalls, scarps, and talus.

Tracks freckled the snow, showing how the herd had milled before crossing a saddle toward higher country. With my binoculars, I could see the way they'd gone. Their trail stretched deeper into the mountains, sidehilling through scree, disappearing among the crags.

The next day was similar: an unbearably cold dawn, elk on far ridges, a long stalk, a near miss, another sighting, fresh hope, a chase, the exhausted walk back to my tent. I saw a few other hunters, but they were far off in lower country. I kept my distance.

I liked that way of hunting—that lupine chasing after wild creatures until my legs shook and buckled—but it didn't work. Each morning, I rose early and saw elk ascending the mountains as if lifted by a rising tide. I followed herds to the limits of my stamina only to have them vanish. Several such days left me with a profound respect for the lungs and hearts of elk and a pressing need to try something different.

Between the forks of Sun Creek, the foothills disintegrate into a jumble of thick-timbered, ravine-cut moraines. It is a roller-coaster terrain of bowls and pothole bogs, with round hills up-thrust like pregnancies. The forks are lonesome, dark, and almost impenetrable. They frightened me when I first came to the Sun.

Though I had ridden around them often enough, I had seldom explored the forks as a ranch hand. They were cluttered with downfall, too steep for horses. A wealth of grass elsewhere usually kept cattle from entering.

Consequently, that corner of the foothills belonged to wild things. Bears denned there, and wolf packs rendezvoused in springtime. The forks were where a hunting guide had gone scouting years before, tripped over something mossy, and excavated from bog muck the largest elk skull ever found in the state of Montana. The half-rotted behemoth made headlines after being measured by awestruck members of the Boone and Crockett Club.

There was something uncanny about the geometry of those old antlers. The main beams stood straighter and more upright than those of any bull I'd seen. Every elk is an ancient, numinous beast, but that giant was something more. He belonged to the Pleistocene and seemed to constitute his own species. The rack was as tall as a person. It was as different from other elk skulls as a cave bear's is from a grizzly's.

Walking farther into a maze of hills and basins, I wondered how such an enormous bull had negotiated such tight forest. I was moving well, though, following a ridgeline, stopping to look into one dell after another. My hunting trip was nearly over. I had gone through food more quickly than expected and had absorbed my fill of cold.

Hollow-stomached and clearheaded, I wanted only to see beyond the next hill. After several days in those mountains, I had come to understand that I was never alone in the wilderness. Fresh snow made this clear. It put a time stamp on everything, proving that animals were everywhere around me—grazing, drinking, bedding down, extravagantly graffitiing the ground with sign. Fresh tracks abounded, each set ending at a living, breathing elk.

That was the humbling thing about the Madison Range: Among thousands of elk and deer, a hunter equipped with binoculars, warm clothes, and a rifle that could shoot from one side of a canyon to the other could go hungry.

Suddenly, there was motion in a narrow clearing below. Cows and calves scattered, wise to my presence, trotting, chirping, braiding their paths around fallen trunks. The brown of them shone warm against the snow. Stepping aside, leaning against the nearest tree, I leveled the crosshairs on the hindmost cow and shot.

My heart jumped after days of silence, skipping a beat then racing like I had been running at full sprint. The elk did not fall, only staggered.

She made for a knot of timber so dense that I wouldn't be able to see or shoot into it. The other cows were already there, vanishing. She was beside the timber, ducking in, when I steadied myself enough to fire again.

Blood hammered in my ears. I hoped that I had hit her well and would not have to chase her through the mountains. I loaded two more shells and crept down from the ridge. All around were melted places where elk had bedded, each connected to the thick timber by a line of tracks. Following those heart-shaped marks into the trees, I found the cow dead.

I was sorry. I was pleased. I stood beside her, grateful and shattered, shaken and cold. When my hands quit shaking, I turned to the task of separating meat, skin, and bone.

From that beginning, I became a hunter. A good one, too, though I am not an exceptional shot. Neither am I terribly quiet or gifted at spotting animals on far hillsides. Instead, I am persistent and made for walking. I know that if a person travels far enough, attending to the animals and country, he will cross paths with something. This doggedness serves better than skill or luck: Over the last fourteen years, in a state where four out of five elk hunters return empty-handed, I have taken a cow or bull whenever I wanted one.

In the course of seeking wild meat, I have crept close to herds and listened to their implausible language of grunts and birdsong. Walking ridges until the rifle's sling cut into my shoulder, I've seen where wild animals sleep and hide. I have learned to trust and preserve my rifle, oiling it against rust, depending on it to keep me safe and fed.

There were years when I lived for hunting in the mountains and the thought of it sustained me in lower country. This embarrassed me at times. I worried that people—my parents and others—might consider me bloodthirsty. Still, the feeling remained. Walking through a forest before sunrise with no other human being for miles, dry snow against my boots and breath the only sound, seemed as necessary to me as food or water.

My godfather, Pat Zentz, once told me that it took three generations to create a complete rancher. This wasn't precisely bragging,
because Pat was only the second generation of his family to graze
the bench and coulee country near Billings. Perhaps he said it because he was proud of his sons. More likely, he said it because he
considered it a fact and was in the habit of telling me the truth.

Ranchers think a lot about lineage. This makes some sense,
since they thrive or fail according to the chromosomal mingling
of cows and bulls. In every valley where I've lived and worked,
there's a story of a local kingpin searching halfway across the
continent for the perfect herd sire and returning with a bull who
threw calves that walked on water.

The same theory gets applied to horses. So pervasive is the
conviction that horses breed true that equestrians will spend
fortunes on airmailed straws of stallion semen. They'll gush
about how that seed, put to their finest mare, yielded colts and
fillies that not only ran like the wind but inherited the entire
mind and soul of their sire.

As with horses, the logic often runs, so it goes with sons and
daughters. Often, I'd pull up to a neighbor's place to see him
emerge from the front door with small carbon copies of himself in tow. At midsummer rodeos, I'd look across the stands at
families arrayed like unpacked matryoshka dolls: There was a

blond set, sitting largest to smallest; over there, a freckled ruddy batch leaning forward at the exact same angle, elbows on blue-jeaned knees.

It wasn't only that kids looked like their parents. They sometimes acted like them, too. A family three generations deep into the craft of breaking horses raised children who excelled at the work. Another displayed a century-long streak of hot temper. I sometimes felt convinced that everything important was heritable.

Here's a story: At a branding, a large community affair, a kid not more than eight walks in among the crush of horses, ropes, and squalling calves. Nobody calls him back. Little straw hat jammed low, he vanishes in dust amid hard-hoofed creatures sure to stamp the life from him without meaning to. He's gone among the legs of horses and the running, working, shouting men of his own and neighboring clans.

Then he appears, hat gone, bent knee jammed into the neck of a prone calf. He tilts back as a man leans in with the red-hot iron and the calf screams, smokes, and thrashes. When the branding's done, the kid lets the creature bound off. He stands, beating dirt from his clothing with thin arms. The man, reaching down, finds the hat in the dirt and puts it back on the boy's head.

"Je—sus Christ!" one fence-leaning oldster tells another. "See him mug that heifer calf? There's his father's boy. Grit like a dry creek in August. Breed 'em that way up here."

Do you envy that boy? For much of my life in agriculture, I did. I coveted such a childhood of rawhide and dust, considering it the opposite of my lot in Seattle. It was a grass-is-greener longing turned upside down. I wanted drought instead of deluge, hard in lieu of soft. I wished to have grown up in a scrum of cattle and horses, and to have been well-started toward manhood while my town-bred schoolfellows were still petting hamsters.

There's a silkscreen print by Andy Warhol called Double Elvis. The piece, derived from a publicity photo for the Western movie Flaming Star, depicts the young, still-thin King as a handsome bowlegged cowboy in the act of a quick draw, six-gun pointed at the viewer.

I saw the print as a child when it came to the art museum where my father worked. It's worth looking at if you ever have the chance. Of course, Warhol, being Warhol, made beaucoup Elvises. This one is part of a series in which the gunslinger image repeats in black ink on a gray backdrop: twice in Double Elvis, thrice in Triple Elvis, and so on. The works are life-size plus some, and there is something compelling about the way one Elvis interacts with another. In some prints, like mine, the figures only touch at the boot. In others, they overlap almost entirely, becoming a wide-chested, two-headed beast.

As a kid, I thought of the image as documentation: Here is a cowboy. Here is his gun. Bang. Elvis.

Once I came to Montana and worked, I saw the print differently. Poser, I thought. See his too-clean shirt, his pompadour that has never suffered a hat's crown. That knife on his belt—let him try to throw a leg across a horse and he'd have to pull the blade from his thigh.

In those days, I was pleased to be a grubby anti-Elvis. An oddly specific pleasure but a real one. Evenings after work, I'd luxuriate in the soreness of my muscles, run fingers through hair sweated flat, and congratulate myself on being the real deal. I carried a folding knife because I knew better.

At such moments, I believed that I had skinned out a lie and come near the heart of something that mattered. Elvis was play-acting. I was not. He was false and I was true.

True, maybe, but never quite complete. I never forgot about my godfather's three generations. His words had landed hard on me, particularly because I heard "complete rancher" as "complete man." He never meant it that way, maybe. I heard it all the same, taking it to mean that I had been born at a disadvantage and would need to catch up.

Back then, I had a simple understanding—as thin as ink on canvas or the play of light onscreen—of how a complete Western man might look, speak, and behave: He would be as tough as bull hide and good with horses, hardscrabble and skilled, competent and unflinching. He'd stand in a way that implied a horse between his legs even when there was no horse. Since I hadn't been born that way, I reasoned, I'd need a teacher.

4

KILLING DEER

THE FIRST STORY I heard about Allen took place in high summer a year or two before I arrived on the Sun Ranch. It involved two guests from the vacation lodge where he worked. The couple, I'm told, was a matched set of self-satisfied one-percenters, opulently overstuffed, a pair of beef Wellingtons made human. After several days complaining about the lodge's appointments—lackluster silverware, absence of a panoramic view from their bedroom, toilet paper of insufficient nap—they ordered up a trail ride.

Allen, the lodge's wrangler and outfitter, took them. In a palm-leaf hat and scuffed leather chaps, he led his clients into the beaked mountains. There were complaints: The woman's mount was untrained, she said. It pulled at the bit. The man had saddle sores and brand-new boots that gnawed his feet.

Halfway across a steep timbered slope, Allen turned in his saddle and saw the man, riding last in line, fall from his horse and roll downhill for twenty yards.

"No reason for it," I remember him saying once. "He just fell. Slid way down in the pines."

Suspecting a stroke or heart attack, Allen jumped to the ground and snubbed his reins to a tree. He was about to start downhill when he heard:

"That fucking horse *bucked*!"

"No," Allen said. "It didn't."

Peremptorily, from his prone position, the man ordered Allen to fetch a truck.

"Can't drive in here."

"Look at him," said the woman. "He's injured."

The guest, gaining his feet, tested one leg then the other.

"I will *not* ride that thing. Call somebody. Use your radio."

Allen replied that no vehicle could reach them. There was nothing to do but get on the horse.

Impertinence, the guest must have been thinking. With all the force he could muster, he shouted up to Allen that he would not be climbing anywhere or riding anything.

As the story was related to me, that was when the man noticed where he was. He looked at the dark timber and uphill at the hard-angled peaks. It was late afternoon. He stood in the shadows where the air already hinted at night's cold.

Glancing back to Allen, the guest found him grinning. Not smiling, exactly, but showing his teeth in an expression that I later came to consider characteristic. Allen made that face when he was hunting and had gotten onto something's trail. The effect was canine, eager, triumphant, and cold. It deepened the creases around his mouth, tightened his lips, narrowed his eyes.

"Come up and ride out," said Allen, after a long complete silence. "Or I'll leave you here, come back tomorrow, and find a big-ass pile of bear shit."

The client was powerful in the larger world. He could hire and fire, and pay people to haul lunch and saddle horses. That was all true and none of it mattered.

Groaning, the man began to climb. It was steep and he came on all fours, clutching saplings, sweating, gasping thin clean air.

Allen watched from his horse, low sun glinting on his wire-rim glasses, that hungry grimace on his face.

This is what I heard about Allen before I met him: He was a horseman and the best hunting guide in the valley. He had broken a rich man's will and made him crawl.

Every rural landscape is leavened with such stalwarts—capable men and women who have conquered bitter seasons and hard times with force, wit, and skill. Allen stood among that elite. In my local pantheon, he was the god of horses and hunting.

Despite the outsize reputation, he was not physically exceptional except for the marks of work and weather. He had big-knuckled hands and gullies descending from his cheekbones to below the corners of his mouth like parentheses. His eyes were pale, as if the summer sky had leached into them. The skin of his face stayed wind-chapped and sunburned all year-round.

Allen's greatest skill was killing wild animals. He had looked long and closely enough at deer and elk to read their minds. His powers were particularly strong on and around the ranch where I worked, where he knew every fold of the land and all the faintest trails. He knew where bulls hid in the mountains and when the good bucks would emerge from the willows.

Throughout my first autumn on the ranch, as I gathered cattle from the higher pastures and drained water troughs in preparation for winter, Allen guided hunters. Early mornings when I started work, I'd see his truck already parked up on a ridge or at the mouth of some draw. I listened as I went about my day for rifle shots—one or two *crack-KOWs* if the client could shoot straight, more if they couldn't.

I wish I could say that Allen and I became friends because we recognized each other as wolves among dogs, but that isn't right. It's true that we were both more feral—each in his way—than other people in the ranch's orbit, but that meant nothing to Allen. We didn't share the valley for long, either. Less than a year after I arrived, Allen quit his job and moved to a small town an hour north.

Just like that, the man everyone asked for advice was gone. He would have vanished from my story, too, if I hadn't been seeing his stepdaughter. She kept Allen in my life after he and I both left the Sun.

I'm not sure what I expected the first time I pulled into Allen's yard—perhaps that I'd find him cleaning a rifle, flensing a carcass, or studying the horizon. Instead, he was stoking a bonfire with the discarded ends of pressure-treated brace rails and threading a hot dog onto a wire skewer. With noisome, too-white smoke drifting up around the outstretched sausage, he greeted me.

I tried to take it in stride. Allen's reputation demanded as much. Still, the fact remained that I had never seen a person cook dinner over wood soaked in copper arsenate. The posts flared and stunk, and I stepped away from the plume.

"Worse shit in these than in them posts," he said, regarding me without visible emotion and passing the package of wieners.

I was conscious of the steadiness of his gaze, sensible to the fact that Allen was the sort of person you took as he was or left alone. Pulling a dog from the pack, I ran it through and held it out to char.

We hunted together for several autumns—always with me tagging along and Allen leading the way. He had a one-ton diesel Dodge, and I remember sitting in the passenger seat, my stomach roiling with too-early food and coffee, the world rushing river-black around us as we tore down the highway. Allen liked setting forth in the godless hours, arriving long before shooting light at whatever trail, river bottom, or ridgeline piqued his interest.

Did we talk on those drives through ink? Haltingly, I recall. Now and then, he flared with old stories: He'd been one of the last trappers and pelt buyers for the Hudson Bay Company, with a territory that ran through most of the Western United States; he and his brother had roped a black bear when they were young and had ridden horses breakneck after freight trains; he had hidden a caged mountain lion from a game warden, talking the warden out of the door of a taxidermy shop while the cat hissed in the back room.

He was a man who looked at bushes before they rustled, not after. When it came to the habits and minds of animals, he could answer questions that I had not even learned to ask. To say that I respected Allen's prowess falls short of the truth. I approached him with something like reverence because his skill at hunting bordered on the supernatural.

Each time we headed out, I tried to learn something new. I followed him through thickets, stepping in his boot prints and doing as he did. When his eyes fixed on something, my whole attention followed them.

What I mostly learned was that Allen won in the end. Animals might elude him once or twice, but each time he gathered infor-mation. He saw where they sheltered during storms and where they liked to night graze. He learned and returned. Because of that, a sense of inevitability accrued to his efforts. When he made up his mind to pursue a herd or stake out a certain field, I ex-pected him to be successful. At the time, I could not have found higher praise for a hunter.

Mostly, we killed deer together around Thanksgiving on a stretch of river floodplain that the state considered to be overpopulated with whitetails. You could buy extra "antlerless" tags for that hunting district, which meant that a person could legally shoot a buck and six does.

Allen and I were hell on those whitetails. It was the easiest and most efficient killing I have ever done. Once, we drove down to the river in the perfect yellow light of late afternoon, the magic hour when even trailer houses are beautiful. Parking the truck on a gravel turnout, we walked—not sneaking but walking with calm purpose—along the bank of a deep half-frozen slough. Allen had a tree stand there, a rickety collection of planks nailed into the forks of a midsize cottonwood.

Climbing up, I rested my shoulder against the trunk, set my rifle in my lap, chambered a round, and settled in to watch the dike that was the slough's only crossing for half a mile. Allen sat on the bole's far side and we kept silent as the sun crept down the sky. When nothing happened for half an hour, I fought to keep from asking whether we should hunt elsewhere. Allen wouldn't hear of it, I knew. Neither would he like me talking in the stand. Patience and an unshakable faith in his plans were among his qualities. When a place looked promising, he stayed through nightfall.

Sunset was burning pink and orange when the first deer showed itself. She slid out of the timber on the slough's far side, walking clear of the trees and making for the dike. The doe paused once to listen. When she stopped again, I shot her cleanly through.

We stayed in the tree and whitetails kept coming. Within ten minutes, a pair of does moved into sight. On Allen's whispered count, we killed them. We were both hunting for other people, getting meat for neighbors who could not do it themselves. A yearling went past, and we let it go. I thought we ought to climb down and gut the deer, and was on the point of saying something when Allen began watching the timber more intently than he had all night.

Something stirred in there. The sun was well below the horizon and I could not see into the shadows. But an animal was moving, working along the edge, jostling branches.

It was late when the buck came into the open. In Montana, the legal shooting day finishes half an hour after sundown. I didn't know what time it was, but we must have been in or past the final minutes. The sky was an empty dark blue, and everything but our fluorescent vests had faded to gray scale. The deer was wary. He stood out farther than I liked to shoot, particularly in low light. Allen nodded at me. With the cottonwood's trunk for a rest, I took a shot that broke the buck's neck.

Allen clapped me on the back, which made me proud. We climbed out of the tree to gut deer in the light of our headlamps. That task, which requires a gory hour of a novice's time, took us not more than ten minutes per animal. We worked in turns—one of us cutting while the other steadied the carcass, keeping it belly up.

Allen had reduced the process to four tasks: First he cored out the deer's rectum with a sharp knife, freeing the lower intestine. Then he cut up along the centerline, slitting skin and fascia, and inserting two fingers—one either side of the knife's drop point—to keep from nicking the stomach. Reaching elbow deep into the rib cage, he sliced the windpipe loose. With the cutting done, he pulled on the trachea for all he was worth until heart, lungs, rumen, and intestines slithered onto the ground.

We killed and dressed four deer in two hours like that, stacked them in the truck like cordwood, and headed home for dinner. Ours was a well-intended slaughter, and I knew people would be grateful for the meat. It did not seem like a bad thing to do.

Allen and I agreed on that much, but there was a difference between us. When I looked at a carcass in the grass—regardless of the people it would feed—I felt some combination of guilt and gratitude. Whether Allen perceived these feelings in me, I can't say. I noticed his habit, though: When he walked up to a deer that he had killed, he kicked it.

I wondered for a while if it was to make sure that they were dead. Sometimes deer play possum. There are stories about hunters beginning the process of gutting an animal only to have the thing lash out or gore them. Allen's habit might have started that way, but with the river deer, it had grown into something else.

That night, he delivered a particularly nasty blow to the first doe. "You bitch," he said in a voice cold enough to remind me that we were standing in the dark with loaded rifles, then he kicked her hard in the face with his boot.

I still don't know if this was a joke or if he meant to teach me something. Perhaps he thought my approach was sentimental or had decided to tempt whatever fates send deer toward a hunter or hide them. Maybe he was proving a point about what went out of an animal with its last breath.

Whatever his reasons, that kick left me wondering whether regret and intentions matter when it comes to killing or if the only real consideration is the hunter's aim.

I'll confess this: My heart beats through my chest every time I draw a bead. The beating, as sympathetic as it is, unsteadies my hand. It doesn't make me miss, but sometimes tremors of conscience pull the bullet inches off its mark, which is enough to make an animal take longer dying.

I don't believe that Allen felt anything for his quarry. His hand was steady and I never saw him take a shot that was anything but clean. Later in the evening, at the dinner table or watching television, he seemed to have forgotten what we had been doing. If he thought about the hunt at all, I believe it was with an uncomplicated satisfaction—the full-bellied contentment of a wolf.

IN THOSE YEARS, I often hunted on the ranch I had begun to manage in the Deer Lodge Valley. The place had been opened to public hunting through a program run by the state of Montana. The plan was to make some extra money—the state paid the ranch a small fee for each hunter—and keep herds of deer and elk from overwintering on the hayfields and the river bottom.

It seemed like a good idea to me. When I signed a contract on the deal, I was thinking about Yellowstone National Park and how wolf reintroduction had restored balance there. How a predator's return kept herds of elk, deer, and bison on the move, spreading their impact across the landscape. After only a few years, new willow thickets were sprouting on Yellowstone's riverbanks, shading water and creating habitat for a great many wild creatures. Overgrazed grasslands regained a measure of health. The ecosystem thrived with hunting pressure.

A version of that, in miniature, is what I hoped would follow from opening Dry Cottonwood Creek Ranch. But human hunters are not like wolves. We are too numerous, our weapons too deadly. Neither can a 2,300-acre ranch, as large as it may seem to the person who mends its fences, stand in for an ecosystem.

All through rifle season, trucks raised dust on Eastside Road, stopping at each high place to glass the river willows and examine the ridges running eastward toward the mountains. There were many, many hunters. As I went about my work, it seemed like a rig was parked or idling at every gate. The state paid ten dollars each time a hunter signed in for the day. Dry Cottonwood hit the program's cap of ten thousand dollars long before rifle season was done.

Game, initially plentiful on the ranch, was quickly overrun. Only a small area around the corrals and barn was set aside from the general pursuit. This safety zone, intended to keep me from taking an errant bullet, became well-known to local deer. Every night and morning, they came into a field behind my barn. I developed a custodial feeling for them. Despite frequent requests, I refused to let hunters in.

One October, I started watching the small herd each evening through a crack between the barn's sliding doors. It was the same deer every night, and the does took a communal approach to mothering their fawns. Sometimes bucks showed up and locked horns. Copying one of Allen's hunting schemes, I hauled three large round hay bales to the field and made a triangular blind.

It worked like a charm. I climbed between the bales before the deer filtered out of the riverside willows and stayed until I could leave under the cover of full darkness. It was often cold and time moved slowly, but I liked watching animals live their lives. From fifty yards off, I saw them eat and laze, and snap to attention at the sound of distant rifle fire. I watched them parse the wind and track movements in the trees beside the field.

Other animals showed themselves. When a place is set aside and left in silence, wild things always come. Coyotes and foxes ran the margins. A porcupine trundled through. Once, bald eagles congregated in the crown of a dead cottonwood tree. First there were three, then five, then eight, then a baker's dozen. All seemed determined to sit in a line on a single gray limb, a feat they accomplished with spread-winged dignity and a good deal of noise. They were beautiful through my binoculars: huge birds with clean white head feathers and cruel beaks perched shoulder to shoulder. It was the kind of scene that gets printed on posters with the word FREEDOM.

As the last bird settled, the branch snapped at the trunk. Eagles fell in a separating, inglorious, screeching mass, taking flight in all directions, some almost hitting the ground. My deer spooked from the field, hid ten minutes, and returned.

Around the time of the eagles, I was in the bale blind on an evening midway through hunting season and had it in mind to kill a deer for a friend of mine in graduate school. I had never shot anything from the blind before, but it should have been easy since the herd had arrived like clockwork with the setting sun to graze fifty yards from where I hid.

One doe stepped clear of the others. She was large and healthy, and stood broadside, offering the wide plane of her shoulder and vitals. She remained that way while I watched her through the scope with the rifle's safety off and my finger soft against the trigger. My rest was as steady as a half ton of baled hay could be, my breathing deep and regular. It was a perfect shot. I could not take it.

She breathed white plumes, working her ears, feeding slowly in a circle toward the others. She was absolutely unaware. Her life seemed very fragile, her survival an unlikely, near-miraculous thing. Perhaps that's what unnerved me.

Soon afterward, I began deceiving hunters. Many came to the barndominium's door to ask how best to stalk the ranch. At first, I answered honestly, telling them how animals moved through the willows and which drainages bucks traveled through from the low country to the higher hills. The hunters listened. They went to all those places and killed deer. My field emptied by degrees.

I remember the first time. I was in the ranch truck, idling window to window with a stranger who had flagged me down on Eastside Road. He was my age and stunk of self-assurance.

"Seein' bucks?" he asked.

"Some," I said.

He wanted to know where. I was gripped by an impulse to steer him wrong.

I described the location of a steep and hideously rocky ravine in the ranch's higher county. The draw boasted neither water nor cover, and was as difficult and deerless a place as I could imagine offhand. I outlined his route, giving mileage and landmarks. I suggested that the drainage was best hunted uphill, a direction that would, with our prevailing wind, surely send the hunter's smell before him.

"Nice mulies," I said. "Up at the top."

That evening, I listened for rifle shots and heard none. Afterward, I recommended the spot often.

"Well," I'd say, as if wrestling a secret. "You might try the gulch."

Having started, it was hard to stop. I had a tree stand in one of the riverside cottonwoods—near the eagle snag—where I'd climb up and sit to watch what went on in the willows. For the most part, the deer needed no help. They were masters of evasion. I liked watching the orange-clad men creeping clumsily through brush while bucks filtered out fifty yards ahead of them, vanishing through gaps in the vegetation. The whitetails made no sound at all. The men were cacophonous. On rare occasions when things started looking dangerous, I'd break off a piece of bark and let it fall. It wasn't a surefire remedy, but the smallest noise made a difference.

Mean pastimes, perhaps, but such betrayals gave me the feeling of being on the right side of something. The hunters had rifles, after all. The animals had nothing but wits and feet.

One morning, I woke and went outside to find the hayfield stubble dotted with gray-brown mounds. *Deer, certainly*, I thought, wondering why they'd bedded so close to the main road in daylight. Only slowly did I grasp that I was looking at a massacre. The pasture between my barn and Eastside Road was full of carcasses—so many that at the start I couldn't grasp what I was seeing. A dozen dead mule deer, maybe more. Does, fawns, and a young buck scattered out from the wayside ditch toward the heart of the field.

Once I knew what I was looking at, I could picture clearly how the thing had happened: The mulies had come down from higher, more secluded hills to night graze on alfalfa, walking unconcerned onto the right-of-way. It must have been dark, well past hunting hours. Then came headlights scything along fence lines, flaring on eyes and pale rumps. The herd ran, but trusting darkness to hide them, the deer did not go far. They bunched and turned.

How was it, I wondered, *that I had slept through the barrage?* The nearest deer was less than a hundred yards from my bedroom window. The fact that I had heard nothing bothered me. It made me feel responsible. When the game warden came, he said that the shooter had probably used a silencer, a spotlight, and a small-caliber gun. There had been other incidents of nighttime poaching. The evidence pointed to a handful of boys fresh out of high school.

At dusk, I stopped work to watch the usual whitetails creep from the willows into the alfalfa field. Turning from their soundless, halting advance, I stared at where the mule deer lay like heaped dark laundry. Two or three trucks passed on Eastside Road while the light failed, slowing abreast of the field. I watched each vehicle out of sight. When a chill settled, I went inside. I kept my house lights low and my attention on the big window that overlooked two miles of county road.

It was a weekend night and people were out. That stretch of the gravel was made for misbehavior, for cruising, racing, assignations, and shooting. For an hour, I watched headlights and taillights speed or creep along according to various purposes. When anyone stopped, I listened closely.

I was washing dishes when a truck came along the road, growled past my barn and corrals, and rolled south. Something struck me about the way the rig was driven—a predatory quality in the vehicle's motion, as if the driver had his boot over the brake pedal, his eyes scanning the shadows. That truck moved like a grizzly does through forest. It looked ready, intent, and dangerous.

A mile off, the taillights flared and headlights yawed around to face my neighbor's fields. It was a black night with fog building along the river. The light was a small white megaphone aimed west. It was elk country down there and I knew what the driver had seen. A big herd descended from the foothills at night to graze alfalfa under the neighbor's center-pivot sprinkler.

Running out the door, I imagined what the poachers could do to hundreds of elk cows and calves. Tossing my grandfather's revolver and a cell phone onto the ranch truck's bench seat, I turned the key and waited while its old engine cranked, guttered, and fired. Halfway out the front gate, I realized that a 1980 Chevy C10 Custom Deluxe—stripped of its muffler, loaded with a quarter ton of barbwire and T-posts, geared low for off-road work—was far from an ideal pursuit vehicle. The pickup was neither quick nor subtle, but I flogged it south down the road as fast as I could.

Headlights on, I could see nothing but the road, right-of-way fences, and tall pale grass at the margins of the beams. Cottonwood trunks flashed past.

I imagined the trigger-happy bastards at work, animals falling in heaps. Just then I could have hurt the poachers, torn into them. I was throttling the steering wheel, shifting gears like a boxer throwing punches. The revolver bounced around when the truck hit potholes, pointing everywhere. I jammed its barrel into the crease at the seatback's base.

My headlights caught a large tan shape at the gravel's outer edge—a cow elk jumping the barbwire. The creature was beautiful in flight, front hooves tucked back, body in a powerful, taut arc. She twisted in midair to watch the speeding truck. I watched her for a moment, too.

When I looked ahead again, the road was full of elk dodging in every direction. I mashed the brake, skidding over washboards, stopping in a dust cloud that rolled forward past me.

Elk were everywhere: spike bulls and cows milling and wheeling; dozens of huge, close wild animals visible in the glare; eyeshine and silhouettes. Dozens more appeared, pouring across and through the right-of way-fences in a pandemonium of hooves and hair. Over the idling engine, I could hear them whistling and chirping, warning one another in their birdsong tongue.

They were all around me. Dust thickened the air, so only the nearer beasts were distinct. For several seconds, none of us knew what to do. Then the more distant creatures—black cutout shapes of wild things—fled upcountry together, leaping headlong away.

The elk numbered in the hundreds, blocking my way, and once

they started flowing across the road in a river of moving limbs and plumed breath, I could do nothing but watch. Keeping still amid the force of that herd was like standing against a rushing stream. I wanted to leave the truck and run with them into the dark foothills.

It was only at the last, when the adults had gone and I sat waiting for the calves to shove and stumble through the barbwire, that I remembered my purpose.

I drove on when I could and came to where the headlights had swerved. The place was not far from where the herd had crossed, and it was empty. No pickup truck. No poachers. No shell casings gleaming in the road. So far as I could see through the mist and darkness, nothing lay dead in the fields.

What did the night poachers of Eastside Road see in all those animals they killed? Was it a game for them? A way to hide for another hour from the future? I made a rosary of those questions, asking daily for months. In the end, I had to stop. To hell with the sons of bitches, *I told myself.* I don't care what they have become, or if they feel heartsick late at night.

To hell with them, really. But you need to know the story and judge it. Then you can ask, as I often have, why they did what they did.

Deer and elk are the least troublesome of animals unless a person plants sapling trees or tries to keep an unfenced orchard. Beyond eating green things, the average deer does little to inconvenience us. She slips along the edges of our world, half seen, quilting browse and stealth into an unlikely life. She is slim-legged, graceful, and unobjectionable. Raising delicate, swift fawns, she teaches them to survive our perversions of the landscape. She thrives where other wild things fail, increasing to such a degree that she may be sustainably hunted almost everywhere that hasn't been paved over. On top of it all, she makes good meat.

I have often wondered how anyone can hold a grudge against an animal of that sort, but some people do. I have met men—always men—who despise the deer they seek each fall despite the fact that doing so runs against all sense and logic. I observed this unreasoned, reflexive hatred not only in killers who prowled East-side Road but in hunters who I respected more. It was in Allen, I think, when he put his boots to the Jefferson River does.

When we walked up to begin the work of gutting out our quarry, I often noticed the shining wetness of a deer's pupils. I thought how diligently that buck or doe had renewed the sheen through the course of life until we stopped her. When we split hindquarters and the fibers of thicker muscles trembled with remnant nervous life, I considered what strength and precision were required to speed a creature over fences and fields. Though I could not have explained it at the time, I grasped the tragedy of shattering what we could not rebuild.

I was alone in these considerations in Allen's company—I'm as certain of that as one person can be about another's inner world—and never spoke my thoughts aloud. I did not ask why he kicked deer, because the question would have marked me as softhearted. I wish now that I had asked him.

Allen and I have long since parted ways. Maybe he is different. It's closing on a decade since we've stood in a field together, and ten years is time enough to change.

I wonder if the anger has burned out of him and where it came from to begin with. I'm curious about the wellspring of that violence. Of this I'm sure: It was rage I saw along the river, a white-hot flaring that ran deeper than his feelings toward any particular whitetail. He was mad about something big. I could feel it. The deer stepped in front of that anger, as if into the path of a truck.

None of this is peculiar to Allen or to hunting. To make a life in ranching means watching people vent their rage on animals. A cowhand hog-ties a cow and leaves her prone on the range overnight to "humble her down." A trucker twists a yearling's tail until it snaps with a crack, then he laughs. A retired rancher, long past owning calves or lambs, hides treble hooks in gobbets of meat to kill coyotes. He goes into the mountains with no object but scattering his deadly morsels and has nothing to gain from the work. Asked why he keeps doing it, the old man pulls a crafty face.

"Teach them not to steal," he says.

Why all this flashing, unnecessary violence? I've kept the question close for years and still lack a satisfying answer. But I know I want to go another way. I want us to go another way. In the course of hunting the Jefferson with Allen, and as I sided with the Dry Cottonwood deer against men who came to kill them, something deep began to rankle. I developed an ache and could not leave it alone. It was like a sore that the tongue's tip revisits until the place grows raw.

At first, I thought my gripe was with bad hunters and so vowed to be a good one. I mostly was. I crept carefully and let some animals escape. My shots were usually clean. But every deer, elk, or bird that I killed in those years cost me something. Every trigger pull made the feeling grow, weighing me down as if I carried some portion of the dead beasts around.

I still liked moving through the mountains and seeing the sun raised and lowered like a flag. I liked watching wild creatures and parsing the crabbed script of tracks. It's only that I came to dread the chase's end and could not stop thinking about how it felt for a deer, standing in tall grass, to receive my bullet.

Once I began to see out of the eyes of animals, I struggled to feel at ease in my life. I could have weathered it better if the feeling had confined itself to hunting, but it did not.

5

BEASTS OF BURDEN

I HAD FEW FRIENDS my own age in the Deer Lodge Valley and seldom got invited anywhere. Because of this, when one of the guys who lived across the river mentioned that he was planning to buck out rodeo bulls on a Friday afternoon, I figured to give it a shot.

My host was a young man who ran a rough-stock company with a few of his friends. They kept Corriente steers to wrestle, calves to rope, bulls, and broncs. Every summer, they'd load a bellowing menagerie into stock trailers and cruise the back highways of Montana, staying one step ahead of the rodeo cowboys who followed the circuit from town to town.

The bulls got tested and, to some extent, trained in the rough art of unseating cowboys before the summer events got underway. That spring day, I pulled up to a set of corrals to find one already in the chute, surrounded by a handful of men in their twenties and thirties.

I knew nobody but the place's owner and had only met him in passing. The men looked clean by ranch standards. Their jeans were snug and very blue, their button-up shirts tucked in and belted. They had their best hats on and were headed to the town bars when their work was through.

Everyone was busy. One man brought a bull up through a network of welded-pipe alleyways; another prodded the animal into the chute and closed a gate behind. Two more guys stood on plank catwalks, hoisted the heavy small metal box of the bucking dummy into place atop the bull's back, and ran a cinch around his belly. The dummy was mounted on a shearling pad. The strap holding it in place ran through a spring-loaded latch set to open at the touch of a button on a remote control.

I hung my elbows across the uppermost rail and watched. The cowboys went about their work quickly, with the competency of old hands. They bucked three bulls in quick succession, each animal spinning through the loose dirt of the arena, jumping and twisting until a tap of the remote control tumbled the dummy off to one side. Sometimes the men nodded approvingly at an animal's exertions.

Even I could see that the bulls were unremarkable. They bucked straight lines and wide circles, just right for August nights and semipro riders. The animals seemed youngish and gawky. Still, they were big enough. The way they dug their horns into the dirt and strained the welded-pipe corrals put an uneasy feeling in my stomach.

Coming into the chute was a large dark-brindled bull of indeterminate breeding—somewhat thicker than the ones before. Everything about him was broad and powerful. A hump suggested Brahman in his lineage, and he had sawed-off forward-sweeping horns. I could not help imagining the horns breaking my ribs, entering my lungs with terrible pressure.

He stood quietly in the chute, a potent beast. I was very close, looking nearly straight down at him. His large shining black eye went wide when somebody cinched the dummy's strap tight. Once, he made a noise between a groan and a sigh. "*Uhhhhunnn,*" he wheezed, and went on standing motionless.

Someone sprung the chute and tugged a rope to swing it open. Late-day sun struck the bull broadside, showing knotted muscles and the bluntly lethal horns.

Now, I told myself, *he will squat, gather strength, and raise dust until his eight seconds are through.* I thought all of this before realizing that I shouldn't have had time to do so. The bull stood blinking in the sun.

"Son of a bitch," somebody said, slapping him open-handed on the haunch. The creature took one step forward. His shoulders were out of the chute, hindquarters still in it.

"Goose him, see what he does," somebody said, and a hand reached forward with an electric cattle prod. I watched the tip reaching out, its forked electrodes like a snake's tongue, and disappearing between the bull's hind legs.

"*Ohh,*" someone whispered. "Right in the *balls.*"

A bellow—one low, sustained, deep sound. The bull showed his strength in a huge leap, rising like a fish breaking clear of water in a heavy black curve, twisting his front hooves aside. Nobody breathed while he corkscrewed upward, hung at the jump's peak for an instant, and started falling. He looked like a poster for the sport only there was nothing riding him but cinches and a metal box.

We thought that was the beginning of the show, but it was the end of it. The bull landed well into the arena on all four feet. He took an easy step forward, felt the tug of the cinch, and stopped. He bent his head around, nosing back along his rib cage to see what the problem might be.

His time was up. The dummy clattered to the dirt and the bull walked off as easy as can be. Raising his muzzle, he called to other cows somewhere. He did it twice, each time a long plaintive call. He listened for an answer. We could hear him breathing in the silence.

"Fucker won't buck," somebody said.

"He's a canner" came the reply. "Too bad. Nice-looking bull."

The bull walked out of the arena without charging fences or menacing anyone. He was gone quickly, down the sturdy alleyways, sorted with the other culls.

I don't remember excusing myself. Everyone was busy bringing animals up through the alleys or putting them away, fiddling with straps and latches or testing the remote control, which had ceased to be dependable.

I drove out the way I had come. I meant to go home but didn't take the correct turns, rattling instead up a road that topped a hill, pulling into green grass where I could see the sun set.

It was a pleasant evening. Winter had fully gone and the grass was rising. *That bull*, I thought, *had a kind eye*. I could still see it as I sat on the tailgate watching the yellow sun drop. His huge pure-black eye had held the unmistakable aspect of tractability; in another time, he might have pulled a cart or plowed fields. He was a fine, calm creature, only he wouldn't buck. For several weeks afterward, I thought of that bull every day.

MONTHS LATER, A COW stayed in the hills after my coworkers and I had gathered all the others, choosing for redoubt a place where beaver ponds ran close beside a thick stand of lodgepole pines. She looked like hell, all skin and bones. All of us who rode the allotment knew she was ailing and dangerous. Having entered a grim part of her prey beast's mind, the sick cow had become murderous.

"She's on the fight," we warned each other. Any time a rider tried to push her into the open, she'd paw, bellow, and charge. As gaunt as she was—ribs like palings, the skin slack across her pelvic bones like an old coat on its hanger—a dire light in her eyes made clear that she meant to shatter anyone she got on the ground. There was no roping her for the trees. The beaver ponds were a moat. Our dogs proved unable to dislodge her.

"It's neurologic," said an older rancher with whom I shared that grazing allotment. "Nothin' you can do. She'll come down on her own or die in there. Die either way."

I returned with a friend to try again. After a long series of charges and retreats, we succeeded in driving her downhill. Following behind, I could see the toll illness had taken. It wasn't just that she was emaciated, though in that respect her condition was as bad as any cow's I've had in my care. She walked as if her limbs disagreed and her mind lacked jurisdiction.

It made for a slow ride off the mountain. Our horses did not understand things, and mine jigged and tugged the reins. When the barn hove into sight, he jostled ahead and bumped into the cow's flank, and she spun and clattered us with her head. She hit hard enough to remind me that even a worn-down cow throws weight around.

Maybe she had eaten poison, or something sharp had perforated her gut. A parasite might have taken hold or some bacterial infection. For all those things, my remedy was the same: plentiful hay, quarantine in the corrals, fresh water, a dose of Ivermectin, and a shot of long-acting antibiotic.

Because I lived beside the corrals, I couldn't come or go without seeing how she was doing. When I broke for lunch, I noticed how she lay in the sun panting. The worst part was that I never saw her drink. A broad ditch ran through a corner of the corrals, and the cottonwoods offered shade there, but she wouldn't—perhaps couldn't—walk the fifty feet from where she lay.

Convinced that if she'd take water she might pull through, I climbed into the corral, dipped a bucketful, and started toward her. There were flies in the corners of her eyes, but she blinked them away when she saw me. Rising, she shook on traitorous legs. The line of her back was jagged with vertebrae and so strikingly echoed the skyline of the valley's western rim, which was behind her, that I was distracted by the likeness. I was bending to set the bucket down between us when she charged.

Charged. The word is right and wrong. She lurched forward but only for two paces. As I jumped back, she pulled up short. Breathing heavily, she regarded me. Her muzzle was hanging over the bucket's rim.

She must smell it, I thought. It was inches from her muzzle and she was dying of thirst. I was cattleman enough to know that much. I looked full at her, willing her to drink, then she charged again, moving like a marionette, knocking the bucket over so water slopped across the hardpacked dirt. She came fast enough, and I was standing close enough, that she nearly caught me.

Backpedaling, I got clear. She stood, panting hard, glaring viciously. The sun bore down. Behind me, quite close, was the ditch and the cottonwoods. We could hear water and the sound of wind in the leaves.

An idea came to me and I took a step forward, halving the distance between us. The cow dropped her head and lurched at me. I dodged back.

I repeated this process, drawing close, provoking a short halting rush until we came to the cottonwoods and ditch. I stepped into the water, feeling it soak through the stitching of my boots. One more charge and the cow was in the ditch, its current lapping her hooves. She seemed to relax slightly. I left her with her head sagging, slack lips inches from the flow.

For three days in a row, we worked through the same slow-motion bullfight. Each time, she was weaker and I had to step closer to provoke a lunge. Sometimes I'd stretch out a hand for her to use as a target. My palm remembers her hot, labored breath.

Three days of dancing toward water. Three days of dragging fresh hay to wherever she lay down. I did everything I could—all that was possible—before realizing that my help had become its own kind of torture.

In the end, I took my grandfather's revolver to the corrals, stood just beyond the range that would provoke her into standing, and stretched out my hand. I was shaking and the gun seemed terribly heavy. She watched me with blank, malevolent eyes right through the moment when I pulled the trigger.

Flies rose and buzzed circles, taking small notice of death. One moment, they were at her eyes, seeking moisture. After the shot's commotion stirred them, they settled back and let the day go on.

It was not that way for me. I felt the revolver kick and saw the cow's head jerk backward. She tipped sideways, shuddered, and lay still. The gunshot went on ringing in my ears—a strange, inimitable noise driving everything from my mind.

I was familiar enough with that sound but not with what followed. While I stood looking down at the cow, the noise opened a new space in me. It was a small black hole behind my eyes, a void that wanted filling.

I thought of my godfather, Pat, sitting at the wheel of his truck, looking across the cab, telling me: "Once, I slipped and fell into a cow's carcass. It was hot and maggots had burst it, and I fell in the fucking middle."

Pat, a man whose toughness I so admired, who raised cattle for slaughter, allowed a moment's pure silence. "Older I get," he said, "the less I can stand the smell of death."

I thought of a neighbor rancher—a kindly man who owned several hundred mother cows on the far side of the Deer Lodge Valley—pointing out a twisted calf in his herd. It had deformed legs and had grown heavy enough that the stumps kept it from traveling to summer pasture.

"Should have knocked him in the head when he was born," he told me. "But I couldn't."

I shot that calf. I did it as a favor, imagining that it would be a lesser burden on me than him.

A car ran up the road, its driver rubbernecking the sight of a man beside a dead cow, revolver in hand. Rousing myself, I got the truck and used a chain to drag her out in the willows. The coyotes came, a bear walked down from the mountains, and deer grazed light-footed among her bones.

LATER THAT YEAR, ON a winter morning, I walked across the barnyard raising a wake of dry snow. The morning was clear and bitter. It was the sort of windless cold that made a pitchfork's wooden handle seem more likely to snap than flex. The animals— steers by a hay bunk, horses in farther pens—might have been statues except for the steam from their nostrils.

I fed the steers, flaking hay from a line of sixteen-hundred-pound bales that stood near the fence. They shuffled forward as I pitched heaps of tightly packed green grass within their reach. Pressing close, they tore into the morning meal. The bigger animals tossed their heads from side to side, claiming the choicest piles.

The steers had thick coats and backs so fat that rain pooled in the dimples at the bases of their spines. They stood exhaling white breath, puffing like furnaces. Haying livestock in December was like feeding a fire because a grazing animal's gut is an engine against cold. I doled out grass and alfalfa, and the animals warmed. It struck me as miraculous, the way a horse or cow with steady rations could thrive.

The ranch's two big bay saddle horses were the picture of health and hardihood. Like the steers, they had grown shaggy and thick as fall played out. Down the fence, they jockeyed for position in the nearest corner of their pen. One broke away trotting, circled round, bit the other on the rump, and sprang back to dodge the inevitable kick. Both shone with energy, hunger, and a rambunctious desire to shoulder through the cold toward spring.

The other horse, the hard-luck one, watched his fellows from a distance. A tall, leggy, registered paint, Salish had been beautiful before he wasted down to skin and bones. One of his eyes was blue, the other brown. Both contained a kindness I have rarely seen in horses. So far as I know, a mean thought never entered his mind.

I hefted a sixty-pound bale of the finest hay, a perfect combination of grass and alfalfa, and swung it over the fence. Months before, I had walked the meadows looking for the right mix of plants, then talked a neighbor into coming over with his little baler—an old machine that cranked out small manageable squares instead of our usual three-quarter-ton goliaths. The results were impressively nutritious and should have carried any herbivore through the dark months.

The bays bent instantly to the task of eating. They snorted and chewed, taking huge mouthfuls, pausing only to move from one pile of feed to the next. Salish, sluggish and bowed, walked unsteadily toward his meal. He dropped his muzzle and picked through stems, eating little. Stretching out, he pissed a dark halting stream that spattered his hind legs. Things had gone awry inside him, and the results were hard to bear. The horse's every move bespoke pain and desperation.

He was rail-thin and skeletal, though I had tried for months to bring him back to his former health with supplements, medicines, and special treatment. All that while, I had hoped that with the right combination of luck, hay, and veterinarians he might persist through winter and strengthen with spring. It was not until December, when the deep cold came and frazil ice descended the river, that I came to my senses and abandoned hope.

I didn't buy Salish. I traded for him, exchanging a fancy aluminum show-horse trailer for nine thousand dollars and a green-broke gelding. The ranch where I fetched him was horse heaven, its outbuildings white-trimmed and beautiful. Compared to where I lived, the grass was fat with water. Sleek mares and geldings dotted the pastures.

I met the owner, who seemed like a decent man. We found Salish near a creek, chewing. The horse was svelte. Not scrawny, exactly, but without the fat I would have expected on a horse belly deep in timothy and brome.

He had a long back, decent withers, and huge, almost perfectly round hooves. I asked about the hooves—whether they held up to the insults of stones and hard ground. The owner didn't know, having only ridden the horse a few times on the soft, yielding sand of an arena.

The horse's sire, a stallion called Norfleet, was one of the great paint studs. His colts and fillies had brought top honors in all manner of shows and competitions. Salish was one of the last sons, born in the wake of Norfleet's final breeding season. Were it not for the fact that he was five years old and lacked training, the owner told me, Salish would be worth thousands.

Head low and ears pricked, he stepped forward and suffered us to catch him. He was calm and seemed to genuinely relish the touch of hands. There was something innately docile, even hang-dog, about his bearing.

Two years after that, on a winter morning, I left Salish and the other animals to their hay, slid open one of the barn's side doors, and went to the backhoe. The engine idled and warmed while I set a log chain and shovel in the loader's upturned bucket.

I rattled out past the corrals and across Eastside Road into a pasture too small to have a name. The soil was bone-dry, coarse, and granitic. Only knapweed and cheatgrass had managed to grow.

I began by peeling back frozen topsoil, cutting a rectangle twelve feet long by six feet wide. Falling into the rhythm of digging, I thought back to the weeks after Salish arrived when I worked each morning on the round corral. All my neighbors knew about the project because I built it in full view of Eastside Road. What they didn't know is that I agonized over each detail of the design and stayed up in the evenings watching videos of famous horsemen, scrutinizing their techniques.

When I finished setting posts, lag-screwed the rough-barked split rails in place, and hung a gate, I brought Salish into the round pen and made him trot circles. We progressed slowly— the process hindered more by my inexperience than any flaw of the horse's. For a week, I worked Salish at the end of a long rope, longeing him around the pen, turning him with tugs on the line. When I added a saddle, he bore it uncomplainingly.

Because I have been hurt by horses, I was afraid when I walked Salish to the center of the round corral, swung my leg across his back, and mounted for the first time. I waited for a storm, an accident, an explosion, but nothing came. He cranked his neck around, looked up at me, and started walking.

I let him find his own way. Once or twice, when the stirrup leather brushed him, Salish broke into crowhops. His bucking was slow and smooth. He never threw me. I don't believe he wanted to.

MY HANDS HAD STOPPED working the backhoe's controls, so its claw hung motionless above the pit. The engine rattled on, filling the morning with fumes. Stirring, I mined through layers of agricultural midden, unearthing metal, bones, and shreds of plastic tarp. Down deep, the man-made objects gave way to cobble.

I remember how the trouble started. We were crossing a high pasture and I felt Salish run out of gas. One moment we were clipping along and the next he went slack, panting, head sagging low. When I climbed off, he nearly tipped sideways then stood weaving like a drunk. I led him the three miles home.

His wasting was a long process because I tried first to deny it, then fight it. I fed so much hay that the other horses grew as round as bowling balls. I wormed Salish, squirting paste down his throat to purge any parasites. I supplemented him with oats and a protein block that tasted like molasses. Through it all, he stayed bony and unwell. The first winter was hard for him. I hung my hopes on springtime.

That May, I turned the horses out in thick new grass. It was good to watch the other two animals slick off; their coarse long cold-weather hair falling away in clumps, replaced by a glossy coat. Horses age each winter. In spring, they become colts again. They find their legs and go ripping around the pasture, wanting only to eat and run.

The bays were reborn, but not Salish. He kept his winter rag-gedness and did not race through the fields. The vet came and left without a real diagnosis. Boluses were given, new supplements purchased, a plan drawn up to revisit his case in a month. By fall, the horse was still unwell. Less remained of him.

I called a vet from another ranching town, a guy with a reputation for saving horses. He listened with a stethoscope to the rumble and shift of Salish's innards, repositioning his hands on the horse's chest and belly. He frowned, straightened, and shook his head. It was strange, he announced. The horse had a heart murmur and perhaps a little sand in his gut, but neither ailment accounted for his emaciated condition.

The vet took blood samples, tucked them into a cooler in the cab of his truck, and promised to be in touch. He was as good as his word. Within a week, he called to say that Salish's kidneys were failing.

The prognosis was bleak. Dialysis was an option, but it meant six months of daily treatment, confinement, and a lifetime of medication. All that work, the vet said, only prolonged the inevitable. With such care, Salish had no more than half a chance of surviving the year.

Knowing what he was getting at, I asked the vet what he'd do in my position.

"If it was my horse," he replied, "I'd keep him fed and put him down the first day he shows a lot of pain. He won't see spring. Winter's going to kill him slow and ugly, or we can do it quick and clean."

Salish dwindled for two more months. He did not seem unhappy. He came to the fences for attention, regarding me with mismatched, guileless eyes, but every morning his progress across the pen was slower. Nothing punctuated the horse's decline, but each day was harder. As winter pressed down upon the barnyard, he faded away.

I was finishing with the backhoe when the vet pulled in. We shook hands and talked about how the weather had snapped cold in the past few days.

"Brutal," he said. "Lot of calls."

Drawing a large quantity of something blue into a banana-size syringe, he admonished me to dig the hole deep. The drugs stayed in the meat. He wouldn't be responsible for the death of scavengers.

I went to Salish in the pen. He stopped licking a tub of protein supplement and dropped his head for the halter. I slipped the lead rope around his neck, fingers shaking enough from cold and nerves that I struggled to knot the halter.

We crossed the road. Salish was loath to leave his fellows, but the vet walked behind, calmly driving him on. Halfway across the small weedy pasture, Salish balked again. I said that we'd gone far enough.

While he readied the syringe and found a vein, I stood face-to-face with the horse. Looking into that kind blue eye, I thought of the day I brought him home. Somewhere past Missoula but far short of the Deer Lodge Valley, I pulled to the side of the highway and walked back to check on my new horse. Inside the trailer was a nervous beast, an animal far outside his comfort zone. Reaching in, I scratched him above the eyes and told him not to worry. I said that we were going somewhere good.

"Stand back," the vet said, but I didn't. I kept my palm against the horse's forehead while he pressed the plunger down. Three seconds passed before Salish folded like a house of cards. He was instantly insensible, gone before he hit the ground. My hand hung in the air as he kicked once, trembled, and went still.

The vet was quickly down the road, leaving a bill and a great cold silence. Looping chains under Salish, I lifted him with the backhoe's loader and drove to the pit. It took three tries to arrange him in a manner that seemed respectful. At last, I got it right, settling the horse so his legs folded and his head lay propped against a wall of soil.

I climbed into the pit to slip the chains. Shifting his bulk to free the links was harder than I thought it would be. He smelled like fresh grass and the malted grain of a protein tub. I memorized his colors and the cloud shapes on his coat. I touched his chipped hooves and tried once to close the staring eye.

THAT YEAR, I TRIED to save the lives of animals and always seemed to fail. It was not just the cow or Salish. A parasite called cryptosporidium swept through the ranch's newborn calves. It was a bad outbreak. The animals shat themselves to death, one after another, while I labored to keep them full of fluids. I lived for a month with a two-liter bottle of warm electrolytes in hand. I spent so much time doctoring that I caught the bug myself, which laid me out for a week. A few calves recovered, but theirs are not the cases I remember well.

It was a hard year, with Salish's passage and the calf plague as capstone. After the horse died, winter landed like a weight on my shoulders. I remember it being particularly harsh but doubt now if the weather was exceptional. The problem was that I climbed into the year's cellar without my usual store of resilience. Like an animal without back fat, I was uninsulated and unprotected. In this condition, I was susceptible to cold and darkness.

For the most part, I was alone. I had neighbors and daytime responsibilities, but my evenings were lakes of solitude. When the sun went down at five, I asked: *Now what?* The ranch had no heated workshop where I could stay busy welding or otherwise find diversion in work. The dog was around, but he was always sleeping in a corner.

I kept to the small world of my barndominium, which felt like a submarine on midwinter nights. Sometimes, I would hold my hand near the window and feel a blackwater pressure beyond the pane.

Like a seagoing vessel, my quarters were trim and sparsely furnished, my possessions few and carefully chosen. Among them was my grandfather's revolver. The gun was often on my mind and in my hands. After I had cooked, eaten, and cleaned up dinner, I'd take the revolver out to oil it or check the action and sight along the barrel at the wall. The weapon seemed important that winter. I kept it loaded, something I had seldom done before.

Pressed as to why I cleaned the revolver so regularly and took it out when I was alone in the evenings, I'd have said that a person must maintain tools and keep them where they can be used. I'd have argued further that it was sensible to keep a weapon handy in the Deer Lodge Valley. The state penitentiary wasn't far away and convicts sometimes made a run for it. The guards, locals told me, only ever put a couple gallons of gas in the trucks that inmates drove on the prison ranch—just enough fuel to bring a desperate man to my barn's door. There were other dangers: bears, lions, and wolves in the mountains.

All true, but so is this: I kept the revolver too close that winter, which is bad practice for a person at low ebb. One cold night after the horse died, I was sitting on the couch, reloading the gun after oiling it with a rag. Looking toward the window's flat darkness, I got to thinking about how he had been there, a trusting kind-eyed horse, right under my hand, trying hard to go on living. He had been with me, warm forehead against my palm, breath in my nose—then gone.

I could not help seeing myself in the way that my horse, brought from kinder climes, had failed in harder country. In those days, I seemed to be falling apart, too. I slept poorly and lacked strength. It was a subtle trouble but unremitting. I saw a doctor. She found nothing wrong except for the fact that my white blood cell count was low, as if I was recovering from some malaise. "Cryptosporidium?" I suggested. The doctor couldn't say.

I was unwell in body and mind. The problem was not simply that there had been a blue-eyed horse and I had watched him die. Neither was it the fact that a cow had come down sick from the mountains and I had brought her water and, in the end, had to shoot her through the brain. In another year, I could have done those things, handled the bad business with the calves, and still borne up to winter.

In other years, I could have done what I had learned to do over the course of working ranches: kill and move on. Grieve briefly and privately if at all. Come to work in the morning. That was the code. It was how things were done.

There's a turn of phrase in cattle country that I call the "halfway" construction. A cowboy may say, for example, that he was "halfway tired" after a hard day of work or "half puckered" when his horse bucked across a mean sidehill. These expressions mute the truth so far as to smother it. The former means that a hired hand was so exhausted that he could hardly lift a fork at dinnertime. The latter is a rancher's way of saying he nearly soiled himself with fear.

I was halfway sick and halfway crazy that winter, finding no joy in my work and little beyond it. The trouble had to do with death: I had tried to save a horse, but the horse had dwindled to bones.

I had brought water to a sick cow but had to shoot her. Neither outcome is rare in ranching. I knew that well enough. The fact that my tragedies were commonplace did not soothe me.

Sometime in the darker months, I began to notice that death was all around me and entirely beyond my control. The knowledge should have made me philosophical. At the time, I just felt numb and oddly careless about life.

It is hard for a cattleman to admit that death is its own absolute master, an eternally unbroken horse, since that fact threatens the basis of husbandry. To make a life of raising animals, he must believe that he can ward off death until its coming suits him. He must keep faith in the precept that if he does certain right things—keeping the calves away from wolves and feeding cows through winter—he will get to choose which animals to slaughter in the fall.

A rancher has to believe that hard work gives him or her the ability to preserve life, that it provides some control over mortality. When that belief is undone, he or she may fall back on more destructive powers.

All that winter, I felt unsettled, faithless, and confused. There came a night when I held the well-oiled revolver in my hand, a strange thought running through my head: I had never aimed a loaded gun at my own foot. Checking carefully that the hammer was lowered and my finger clear of the trigger, I did so. Looking across the bucktoothed sights at the thin metatarsals ridging my sock, I thought how beautifully complex a foot was and how irreparably it could be shattered. It was terribly easy to point that handgun at things—my knee, my thigh. Without so much as straining, my right hand turned it on my left. It cost no more effort than a gesture.

I understood it then. As one hand threatened the other, I realized that I had stumbled across the only sure way to take the reins of death. There ensued an awful stillness in which I thought seriously about self-destruction for the first time in my life. I had known the magnetism of the void before when I stood looking from the rims of cliffs. Everyone feels that pull and knows the thrill of resisting it. This was different and more dangerous. I had never seen so clearly how the thing was done and why people did it. I had never entertained such thoughts with a loaded weapon in hand.

The dog eyed me from his corner. I remember that. He watched critically, carefully, skeptically. He disliked guns. He raised his head to fix me with a stare.

Slipping the catch that let the revolver's cylinder swing out, I ejected the cartridges and counted six rounds in the hollow of my palm. I counted twice and checked the chambers to make certain that the gun was empty. I put the thing aside—threw it on the kitchen counter—and removed the bullets to the room's far end. I wanted to separate the two halves of gunfire with physical distance, as if a live shell might creep home.

I felt unclean. For a moment, I did not know what to do. Then I stripped my clothes away—jeans, socks, shirt, pants, long underwear—until I stood pale and naked before the glass door's black mirror.

I stepped outside. The night was as frigid and sharp as glass, with a skiff of weightless snow. The stars were clear and bright, and the porch's concrete stung the bare soles of my feet. It was the kind of cold in which pipes crack and a dry leaf, touched, shatters. The upper atmosphere had vanished, leaving nothing between the earth and space. Magpies clustered in the nearest trees. If they could have seen heat rising from me, I'd have burned like a shooting star.

Good sense commanded me to go indoors, but I held fast,

shifting from one leg to the other until my feet numbed. I stood still, thin arms over bare chest, and pulled drafts of air for what seemed like a long time. My skin pricked and stung with cold. Every muscle knotted. The door behind me glowed, but I did not turn. I looked into the darkness, shivered, and listened to the sounds of heavy animals moving—horses in corrals, cows in fields.

I cried fiercely, wildly, in a way that would have terrified a passerby. At first, I had no idea why. My eyes were shut, and behind them, I could see the horse falling dead, leaving my hand alone in the air. I glimpsed the cow that would not drink, her poll in my pistol sights. There was the bull that would not buck, rising once beautifully into the sky, then walking to the cull pen. I saw an endless succession of calves—sick ones that I had failed to save, healthy ones I had shipped to feedlots. I saw deer and elk falling to bullets. All those creatures filled the dark and I cried over them like a brokenhearted child.

Like anyone who grew up on Western movies and books, I learned early how a man is supposed to meet certain varieties of death or peril. Perhaps you learned it, too, but here's the gist: When the black-hatted desperado calls you out, meet him in the street. Make your stand and fight until you fall.

If there are situations when that training and those notions are useful, I haven't yet run across them. I've mostly encountered death and loss in uncinematic forms—experiences that leave me wondering less about confronting the reaper and more about how to carry the weight that remains when he's gone. I have questions about grief and how to bear it. For that, our films and songs have fewer answers.

I used to believe that the proper response to such pain, particularly for a man of my profession, was to shoulder it and press ruggedly, uncomplainingly, solitarily on. A lot of people think along these lines. Some of them carry such burdens of unprocessed sorrow that they are ground into the West's dry and scenic dirt.

I want you to know about a rancher in the Deer Lodge Valley, a man exactly my mother's age, who showed me a different way. Ted and his wife, Julie, had several children, all but one of whom survived to adulthood. The other son was born with a developmental disability that kept him close to home, tightly *under his father's wing. Ted took him everywhere. In telling me the story, three different neighbors used the word* inseparable *to describe father and son. In his late teens, the boy died. That was several years before I came to Deer Lodge.*

In our part of the valley lived another young man with a similar disability, once a playmate of the rancher's son. Ted often brought Casey, who was in his midtwenties by the time I arrived, along when we stacked hay together. Partway through every afternoon of that work, Ted would sink the forks of his open-cab backhoe into a huge bale and bear down on the hydraulics until his front wheels lifted high off the ground. The machine reared like a horse. Sitting on the fender, holding on for dear life, Casey would scream with a glee so pure and powerful that it makes me happy even now. They had bucked the backhoe that way, perhaps, since Ted's son and Casey were kids.

It was dangerous but also a form of magic. That game—a thing the two of them could only do together—conjured a missing child, a departed friend. It worked so well that at times even I, who never met the son, could almost see him sitting there laughing. On such days, there was nothing tough, heavy, or melancholy in Ted, only a joy and resilience that I have ever since admired.

6

THE YEAR I DIDN'T HUNT

LIKE A DEER STRETCHING out to run, I must cover country. I left Dry Cottonwood Creek for another ranch in a hanging valley that looked like paradise. The mountains there were Clovispointed and entirely wild. Years passed and I made little progress toward understanding the feeling that dogged me.

The blessing and curse of agriculture is that there's always something to do. Life is breakfast, work, and dinner; sunrise, heat, and vivid stars; the turning seasons and a good dog running fast through knee-high grass. When the world contains only that much, it is very nearly full. Then there are machines to fix, hooves that need trimming, and bulls to buy from other indefatigable men and women.

If he or she wants to, a rancher can vanish into work as if into a whirlwind. Done well, the trick collapses time. A week can pass or a season. True masters of the art stay gone for a lifetime, emerging only in their twilight years as stove-up ghosts who haunt the backroads in one-ton diesel wheelchairs. They call sixty-year-old pillars of the community "kids." The kids are seldom up to snuff.

I was not such a complete rancher. Every time winter came around, the whirlwind let me down. Then I could not shake the feeling that I had gone wrong somehow, that my good life had turned on me. I wondered why but could make no headway with the question except to say that doing certain things turned my thoughts in dark directions. Hunting was one. Sending calves to the feedlots in late fall was another. Holding my grandfather's Smith & Wesson was worst of all.

For the life of me, I could not understand why my hands trembled like aspen leaves before I pulled a trigger. I could think of no good reason why standing over the year's buck or elk should leave me feeling criminal or why picking up my grandfather's gun engendered fearful thoughts.

But that was the way of it. I'd be out riding horseback in grizzly country with the revolver on my hip, and the idea of self-destruction would slip up behind me like another rider on the trail. I'd carry the gun when I went into the woods to haul out quartered deer and elk, and the bad idea would lurk in the brush. I resisted it. I always believed that I could.

Telling it straight, I'd have to confess to thinking at times that my grandfather's gun wanted to do me harm. It didn't matter how many times I reminded myself that the weapon was only metal and wood, a thing no more capable of desire than a river stone. I fortified myself, but the sense of intention remained.

I probably should have talked to somebody. Instead, I left the ranch in paradise and let time pass. I moved to Missoula and hid the Smith & Wesson away in the basement of a little house I bought. I made these choices out of a dim sense of self-preservation, in the face of something that I would then have called exhaustion. It was instinctive: I recoiled from aspects of my former life, the life

I'd dreamed of as a child, as if I were jerking a burned hand from a stove.

After I moved to town, I did not look at the weapon or think of it. That was easy to do because my life had changed.

Thirty miles east of Missoula, topography presses Interstate 90 close against the Clark Fork River. Road and stream pass into a narrow winding canyon of fractured red-streaked bedrock. Every time I drive that stretch and see the river tonguing stone, I'm reminded that the Bearmouth is aptly named.

It is a deadly place in winter. Stubborn in freezing, the Clark Fork breathes steam across the asphalt. In a fog or wet snow, black ice gleams on the highway. Streaks of paint on the Jersey barriers are the only colors. I drove through the Bearmouth often when I ranched near Deer Lodge, enough to remember the locations of the small white memorial crosses by the wayside.

One night, heading for Missoula after dark in one of early winter's uglier blizzards, I rounded the first blind curve and barely missed a crumpled station wagon. I passed within three feet of it, tires skittering. The small sea-green car sat midway through the turn's apex, straddling both westbound lanes. Its cab was dark and still, which put a sinking feeling in my stomach.

Heavy flakes stuck and clumped on my shoulders. There was a gibbous moon above the clouds, its dim light everywhere around me. While I skidded to a stop on the shoulder, a tractor trailer roared into the turn, locked its tires, and fishtailed. As it passed, I could see the trucker's face lit by the instrument glow, his mouth a worried line as he found a gear and hit the gas anew. After he disappeared into whirling snow, I could hear the sound of another diesel faintly from the east.

Hurrying over the slick pavement, I went to the car and found its driver alive, in shock but unhurt. I do not remember what we said to each other because the distant engine's noise had grown louder and was ringing in my ears.

There was nothing to do but get the car off the road if we could. The first semi had missed it only by inches and the storm was getting worse. Because the driver was rattled, we arranged it so she sat in the car's passenger seat and I was behind the wheel. When I turned the key, hoping that I wasn't setting a match to spilled gasoline, the engine lugged for several seconds but refused to run. In the ensuing silence, the sound of the oncoming truck was louder than before. I glanced across the cab, scared. We were two strangers about to die on a highway in a car that did not start.

I tried again, this time mashing my foot down on the clutch and twisting the key so hard I could have broken it. The motor cranked, caught, and fired as the glare of headlights caught us.

I heard the truck's transmission gnash its teeth in a downshift then the tearing sound of rubber losing purchase on the road. There followed a horrid, still moment of anticipation. The falling snow was thick enough that high beams set the whole air glowing.

The rig's bumper passed close in a blur of chrome, throwing wind enough to shudder the car. Everything went taillight-red as the tractor trailer slid, began to jackknife, straightened, and sped on. I put the car in gear and gave it lots of gas. It lurched onto the road's asphalt shoulder with a grinding sound.

While the wrecker drove up from Missoula, the shocked driver and I sat in my car and talked. It was nearing Christmastime. On a long drive home from Arizona to Kalispell, she'd stopped to buy a good bottle of red wine as a present for her father. When the ice spun her and the station wagon struck the concrete divider, that bottle flipped like a bowling pin from behind the back seat, hit the windshield, and came to rest unbroken on the dash. Sitting in my car, watching wet flakes come down, we pronounced this miraculous.

Since that night, I have been fascinated and troubled by how quickly and completely life can change. An image remains with me of two sparks traversing a huge darkness then converging. As big as this world is, I have wondered many times what the odds are of coming together. Of meeting a dark-haired, bright-eyed woman that way, seeing her depart in a tow truck, then crossing paths months later on a mountain path outside Missoula. Of walking into town together, finding a bar, and dancing until the band wears out and the house lights flicker. Of waking up one morning to find that she—a woman whose lips are always dark as if she has been eating berries, a woman of uncalculating kindness and excellent luck—stands precisely at the heart of life.

Vanishing odds, but it went that way. Four years passed. While Gillian and I lived together in Missoula, I did not think of my grandfather's gun, or ranching, or anything much except the joy of looping an arm across her bare shoulders and squiring her through the world.

But I wasn't made for town. She wasn't, either. When things fell into place and we found ourselves with one chance to buy a farm north of Missoula, we boxed our things. I came up the basement stairs with the revolver in its zippered case. Gillian asked what was inside.

She looked it over and might have picked it up. What I remember is that the gun made no lasting impression. It was a relic, like the saddle gathering dust in our garage or cowboy hats that fit too snug with longer hair.

Off we went, hauling a trailer load up Evaro Hill, crossing onto the Flathead Indian Reservation and into the Jocko Valley. The farm was private land, though it lay within the boundaries of the

reservation. Like thousands of similar parcels, its tribal ownership
had been terminated in 1887 by the General Allotment Act, a
nefarious federal law allowing for the sale of treaty-protected reservation land to white settlers. The Dawes Act, as the legislation
became known as, was hell on the landholdings of the Confederated Salish and Kootenai Tribes of the Flathead Reservation.
Contemporary census results make this clear: Of the Flathead reservation's 28,000 residents, only around 5,000 people are enrolled
members of the tribes.

In the case of our farm, legal title to the ground had been
owned by newcomers for a century. It had passed through many
hands before coming into the possession of the kindly older couple who offered the land to us.

Asking ourselves if we could move to the reservation without
doing wrong, Gillian and I reached no clear answer. We talked
about it often, our conversations always following similar lines:
The past was compromising. The land was beautiful and rare—a
chance that comes once in a lifetime. We knew that someone else
would buy the farm if we did not. We knew that the buyer would
not be the Confederated Salish and Kootenai Tribes.

I asked a friend of mine, a tribal member named Germaine, for
her opinion. She said that history was unjust and unchangeable,
the Dawes Act a form of large-scale robbery.

"There are people who move here and are hostile to the tribes,"
she told me. "That's incredibly unfortunate. But the people who
come because they see what we have done—that we have Class 1
air and water quality, and we're a nuclear-free reservation—those
are people I'd rather welcome."

Germaine went on, clarifying that she was not throwing a door
wide open to anyone with good intentions. The reservation was
full, she told me, and too much habitat and fertile land had al-

ready been lost to subdivision. Put simply: Moving to a farm was fine. Parceling and paving it was not.

Gillian and I bought the place, promising each other that we would be good neighbors. To us, this meant sharing the food we raised, keeping the land healthy and open, and respecting the sovereign rights of the Confederated Salish and Kootenai Tribes. We swore to do these things, always wondering if they amounted to enough.

It was a mountain farm. There were nearer peaks immediately east and south of us. Taller ones, the Mission Range, formed the valley's northern horizon. There were many unnamed summits and also the truncated hump of McLeod, the haystack of Gray Wolf, and the schooner rigs of East and West Saint Mary's.

The closest ridges were steep enough to look like they might tumble into the valley. To judge by the car-size chunks of stone in our fields, it had happened before. Except for the pinnacles and talus, the high country wore an unbroken timber shroud. That forest ended precisely at the farm's southeast corner. It used to descend farther: Our uppermost pasture contained six huge ponderosas that had survived decades of timbering and grazing, and two gray snags that had succumbed but had kept upright somehow.

The land had long ago been cleared for cattle—our only remaining thicket was behind the farmhouse that Gillian and I moved into—but the farm faced the woods. The land's sweep drew a person's gaze toward the foothills, where pines and undergrowth pressed against our fence like a barricaded crowd.

The wires and posts held the trees at bay but not wild animals. Even before we took up residence on the farm, we knew that creatures passed through. There were foxes and coyotes, many skunks, and deer. Hawks seemed always to be crossing our corner of the sky.

I had taken a job with a conservation group that aimed to make an unlikely peace between large carnivores and ranchers. In that capacity, I set out trail cameras, bought livestock guardian dogs for shepherds at the end of their wits, and built electrified fences that would send even the most persistent bears running back into the mountains.

I did much of this work in partnership with the natural resources department of the Confederated Salish and Kootenai Tribes—the peoples for whom the Flathead reservation is reserved—and so learned that a young radio-collared grizzly had bedded in the aspens behind our farmhouse. I loved the thought of that: the great bear sleeping fifty yards away.

We worked hard at stripping rotten siding and replacing broken windows. We talked a neighbor into plowing us a garden. The farm was small by my former ranching standards—a square of nearly 160 acres, measuring a half mile on each side—but amazingly productive. Half the land had been planted in hay, the rest was pasture. Using a network of rough but functional ditches, we could flood almost every square foot of ground with irrigation water.

That first summer, we grazed a neighbor's cattle on our pastures for cash and talked about starting a herd of our own. Our days were long. I fell into bed each night with heat still radiating from my skin, leaning up on an elbow while Gillian slipped from her clothes. A familiar whirlwind caught and carried me so the weeks and months ran together in a joyous marathon.

Autumn came as a surprise. A week before Thanksgiving, a storm caught me cutting firewood in a neighbor's forest. Wind sharpened and hissed in the branches. Driving out with my truck loaded down to its axles, I peered through slanting snow into the woods. The neighbor's place was perfect whitetail habitat, with trickling springs and clumps of aspen. *Soon*, I thought, *the deer would rise from daybeds, shake off the chill, and move toward grass.*

Once the snow came, I felt like hunting. That impulse comes every year. It is separate, somehow, from how I feel about killing. It arrives with a punctuality and strength that I recognize as innate. When the mornings turn crisp and clear, I start peering closely at ridgelines and deep into forests. This shift in attention does not feel like a choice. It just happens. That time of year comes, and no matter my plans, I track the movements of animals. I stalk them in my mind.

Elsewhere in Montana, the opening day of rifle season comes with a fusillade. Hunters skulk through drainages that have lain unexplored for months. Taking positions on nameless ridges, they wait for dawn and movement. The deer and elk are poorly prepared, having grown careless through spring and summer. The result is a running skirmish in the hills.

Our farm is spared this because it lies within the boundaries of the reservation. Only tribal members can hunt deer and elk, and since they do so year-round, there is no autumnal orange-vested rush for the hills.

There were deer everywhere on our place, as there always are on farms with hayfields. I knew some of the regulars by sight: the clueless yearling with a fork horn on one side of his head and nothing on the other, four does that ran together, a careful mother with twin fawns.

And there was the buck. I first saw him while I was up running old logging roads on the tribal land behind our place. We crossed paths on the neighbor's ranch a few days later, and as he trotted into the brush of Agency Creek, I knew that his antlers had grown into a liability. He was, as people say, a shooter. I never wanted to kill him, though.

Still, I thought I might go hunting somewhere. Since I had lived in Montana, I had not missed a season or lacked for winter meat. One spot particularly tempted me: a steep ravine that I passed every time I drove to Missoula. It was a few miles off the reservation, and in November, there were often trucks parked beside the highway. Once, driving up Evaro Hill toward home, I saw two men walking uphill into the timber. I felt a pang of envy. They would see deer from a distance and know the joy of creeping. They would parse the high country while I remained below. *Why shouldn't I go?* I thought, as I turned onto our road.

The following morning, I saw the buck bedded in a copse of sour-cherry trees just northwest of our house. His ears and the wide basket of his antlers showed clearly above the grass and weeds. It seemed strange that he would take cover so near our porch and that the front door's sound hadn't sent him running.

He looked north across the fields, declining to notice me. I took a roundabout path to the shed. Two days later, our pie-cherry trees were full of birds. A dozen magpies perched in higher branches, several ravens waited lower down, and a pair of bald eagles stood in the grass looking intently at something. The birds took flight in a raucous crowd. A coyote lifted his head from tearing at a haunch and bolted through a hole in the fence, running full tilt across our pastures toward the mountains.

The buck lay in a circle of trampled wet snow. Bird shit flecked his coat and the coyote had eaten into one of his hams, but otherwise his body was intact. Reaching down to haul him farther from the house, I took his foreleg in hand. As I began to pull, I recognized the grating freewheel of a shot-through shoulder. I saw the entry wound—a small mark forward of the vitals—only a few inches separating it from what would have been a perfect shot.

Dragging him as best I could, I towed the buck uphill toward the highest corner of the farm. The snow was thin and wet, good for skidding, and the carcass left a trail from the yard to the old ponderosa growing nearest to our fence line and the mountains. I meant to leave him and go on with my day, but found myself examining the ruined shoulder.

The wound was tiny and without an exit hole. A small-caliber gun, then; a rifle just strong enough to break bone. I seldom saw maimed deer on the reservation because most of the tribal hunters were good at killing cleanly. Having year-round access to animals that saw little hunting pressure, there were few reasons for them to take a poor shot or hunt deer with a rifle better suited to gophers. Whitetails are less skittish here. They still fear humans but do not sprint for the horizon as readily as off-reservation deer.

Though I could not know the truth of what had happened, I imagined a white man rattling his pickup along the irrigation canal road that cuts through the forest above our farm. Maybe he had taken the scenic route home from work in Missoula or was just cruising, as people do.

Seeing the buck, he could not resist and pulled his varmint gun from where it hung in a rack and steadied it on the doorframe. The forest is thick up there. A small-caliber shot would not carry far and the canal roads were almost always empty. If the buck proved too heavy to load in a hurry, he could take the backstraps and head, then split—drive home with a wall hanger and good steaks, nobody the wiser.

Maybe the window ledge wasn't a good rest, or the gun didn't shoot true, or the buck shied as the firing pin snapped home. Before the man could rack a second cartridge in, the deer was gone behind curtains of snowberry, dogwood, and vine maple. Did he know that he had hit it? Did he walk out to search for blood? In the end, as I imagine it, he set the rifle in its hooks and traveled on.

No matter how the thing unfolded, it ended with the buck plunging step by shattered step through seeps and forest to our farm. I wondered how he could have leapt five barbed wires in his state.

He found the island of timber surrounding our farmhouse, the same grove in which a grizzly had sheltered. It wasn't much, just a horseshoe of trees and brush twenty paces across. Perhaps it was the best cover he could reach in his condition, or he couldn't press on. He spent time beneath our cherry trees, then died.

I looked at the buck closely, focusing not on the wound but on the rest of him. He was a beautiful deer where scavengers hadn't touched him, with heavy forward-swept antlers and a neck so wide and densely furred that it looked leonine. *A waste*, I thought, though the birds would waste nothing.

Withdrawing, I sat in thin wet snow, watching the magpies swoop, chatter, and land on the red-fleshed haunch. They fed unceremoniously, tilting their heads one way then another, pinching shreds of meat and tipping their beaks toward the sky.

It was a poor day for sitting. My pants soaked through and my cheeks went numb within minutes. Still, I stayed. I sat looking at the deer, my mind on bullets.

Even a small round does a shocking amount of damage. Every hunter who has opened up a shoulder-shot ruminant knows this. Bones explode like pipe bombs, scattering shrapnel. Bloodshot—a dark, jellied, subcutaneous hemorrhage—extends in all directions. For years, I had been cutting that ruined flesh away from my kills. There were times, as I butchered on a cold, pretty hillside, when I came close to foreswearing meat.

Sitting near the buck, I could not stand the prospect of watching anything wild and beautiful through a rifle scope. I did not want to pull a trigger. I resolved not to hunt that fall.

Eschewing big-game season, I had no need to take practice shots or undertake the yearly cleaning and oiling of my guns. I waited, putting off that latter task until the dead of the year—those weeks of late December when summer seems less like a real memory than a story someone told.

IT HAD SNOWED IN the night and morning pressed a fog against the windows. I was used to being alone, because Gillian worked in town, but that day was more solitary than most. The weather was still, the light white and directionless, the silence of a sort that wanted breaking.

I retrieved my guns from the basement room where we keep gear, carried them upstairs, and laid out the armory on an old sheet across the kitchen table: the twelve-gauge shotgun for hunting ducks; the .22 bought before anything else because it was the cheapest way to practice shooting; two hunting rifles, one a levered .308 and the other a bolt-action 30–06; my grandfather's Smith & Wesson.

My godfather, Pat Zentz, told me long ago that a gun was a tool like any other. For years, I used those words as a kind of justification. On that white-lit winter day, a question occurred to me. *If these are tools,* I wondered, *what, precisely, is each one of them for?*

The question was easy to answer for the long guns. The .22 was for practice, the twelve-gauge for birds. The two larger rifles were purpose-built for hunting deer and elk. Those rifles had sent me walking in the hinterlands. They had fed me through winters, tying me to the epic round of life and death that unfolds in wild places. For the most part, my use of those guns matched the purposes for which they had been designed.

The revolver differed. Its cartridge, the .357 Magnum, was developed for the Federal Bureau of Investigation in the 1920s.

With bootleggers and bank robbers making savvy use of automo-
biles, officers wanted a round that could punch through a steel car
door or a bulletproof vest with enough velocity left in it to snuff
out the life inside.

All guns are made for killing, but a handgun chambered in
.357 Magnum has a yet more specific purpose. It wasn't invented
for deer or ducks. Before that morning, I had never looked at my
grandfather's black-shining, beautiful revolver and told myself the
simple truth: This thing I keep and carry is built for killing people.

———✦———

"A guy buys a backhoe," a rancher friend told me. "And every piece of ground starts looking like it needs a hole."

In other words, tools demand their proper use. A hammer seeks nails. Saws want wood. Knives crave something to carve. By offering its particular set of possibilities, each tool makes us an offer. Hammer and saw, for example, promise the shelter of a well-made house. A knife offers succor, a piece of steak on the tongue.

Our tools tempt and work on us. Often, we find them irresistible. I first came to suspect this while shipping cattle.

On a shipping day—usually a pretty autumn morning—a semitruck backs up with airbrakes hissing to the four-foot-high load-out ramp of a corral. The driver is already behind schedule. That's the nature of hauling. The daylight hours are seldom long enough for a person to arrive, sort unruly animals, load fifty-odd mother cows or sixty-odd calves, drive to their destination, and reprise the task in reverse.

Loading can be dangerous work because no range cow worth her salt wants to climb into a metal box and cruise the highway. Still, every one of the beasts must go. The job requires force and patience, a combination of bullying and persuasion. It begins with sorting off the right number of animals for each of the trailer's compartments.

"Three sevens, then thirteen, then a jag of eleven," a driver might shout as he opened the trailer's rear guillotine door.

I'd cut that many from the herd and walk them up the alleyway until the trucker stepped in behind them and sent the leader up the ramp. Sometimes this worked like a charm—the lead cow vanished through the door and the rest of the gang followed in a clatter of hooves on steel. More often, one balked or backed down the ramp double time.

Over fifteen years of loading stock, I watched dozens of people solve the problem of a cow refusing the trailer. The ranchers and truckers tried many things with varying degrees of success. There was only one unfailing constant: When the herder carried something in hand—whether it was a stick, a whip, or an electric prod—the goad got used before the job was done.

The rule held as true for me as anyone. In the moment of striking at or shocking a cow, the act always seemed necessary, the tool's use inevitable. No way around it, *I'd tell myself as I took a swing or hit the button.* Stubborn old rip.

Then again, I've loaded cattle without electric prods, poles, or whips, and the task ended up done. I've loaded semis with a scrap of irrigation tarp as my sole means of persuasion. When cattle balked on those days, I found other ways to send them on. Sometimes, all it took was patience.

7

MAKING ROUNDS

BASS'S GUN RACK IS located in a strip mall in central Missoula, its storefront advertised by a hand-drawn logo of a huge elk rack with a rifle hung across the brow tines. When I pulled up in front of it, the only other decor was a window mural—left over from the Christmastime rush and weathering toward permanence—of a bull elk and an Elmer Fudd–ish hunter. The hunter faced away from his quarry, scanning the street with a cartoon rifle held ready. That he hadn't seen the elk seemed implausible with the two of them on adjacent panes, nearly touching.

But for those two figures and a paper sign reading SENATOR JON TESTER SUPPORTS ANTI-GUN MEASURES, the facade was dark and empty when I pulled up. It was early afternoon, midweek, but the place looked closed.

I had come because I remembered Bass from when he worked at Sportsman's Surplus—a local shop where I used to buy remaindered woolens, propane canisters, and other things related to camping, fishing, and hunting at a fraction of what they cost at chain stores. Bass ran the gun counter—or at least was behind

it holding court every time I went in—and possessed an encyclo-
pedic knowledge of all things related to firearms. He or one of
his deacons sold me my shotgun and both of my hunting rifles.
When Sportsman's folded in the late aughts, Bass went it alone.

Having driven in thirty minutes from the farm, I resolved to
try the door in spite of its unpromising aspect. I took a canvas bag
from the seat behind me, squinted through glass, and found that
I could make out several figures. One of them was waving me in.

The store was smaller than I expected, a single room perhaps
forty feet square, with double-decker gun racks covering every
wall. Lights were on, but the overall impression was of dimness.

Four people were in the shop that day and they all paused to
watch me come in. Bass wore a camo shirt and oil-streaked pants,
and appeared to have done nothing but gray and wrinkle slightly
in the years since I had seen him. He stood beside a glass-topped
counter where a revolver lay in pieces. A big guy named Donny,
who I also remembered from his Sportsman's Surplus days, sat behind the counter near the register. Two customers stopped browsing the racks, glanced sidelong in my direction, and recommenced
perusing.

Pulling the .357 from the bag and passing it to Bass, I told
him that I wanted to learn what I could about a gun from my
grandfather.

He turned the weapon one way then another, then flipped the
cylinder out to peer at a serial number stamped into the steel.

"This's a nice gun," he said, eyes still on the revolver. "Helluva
nice gun."

He had the slow, nearly Southern way of talking that is common in certain rural circles hereabouts.

"Smith & Wesson. Five-eighty-six, ain't it?"

"Dash one, looks like," Donny said.

"Five-eighty-six dash one," Bass confirmed.

"Nice," said Donny.

"Hold its value," Bass went on. "Built on the K-Frame. Wood grips. Target sights."

He pointed out the weapon's length and the heavy metal rod along the barrel's keel. "It's a shooter's gun," he said. "You can set this thing dead-on—any kind of ammo."

"Helluva lot better," Donny added, gesturing to the counter, "than this here."

Bass grunted. "Got that right. That's a damn Clinton gun."

"Bill Clinton. See this here?" He pointed to a tiny aperture in the frame between the trigger and hammer.

"Takes a key. There's the feds for you. You can lock this so it won't shoot no matter what. Clinton's boys thought that up, sons of bitches."

"You remember?" He looked at Donny. "We sold a shitload of these at Sportsman's. The boss bought 'em."

There followed a short silence. When it passed, Bass looked straight at me for the first time since I'd handed across the gun.

"What you want to do with this?"

I told him that I was deciding whether or not to keep it, and asked what the revolver was worth.

"Your grandfather gave it to you?" he said, disapproval edging his voice. "I guess he'd want you to get the most out of it that you can. And if that means selling it, fine. But if that means keeping it, I'll tell you something. This gun here's always going to be worth what it's worth. I mean it's not going to fall off any. If its $550 this year, it'll be $550 ten years from now. That's the thing about a good gun—it ain't gonna depreciate. This here is money in the bank."

He asked if I wanted to leave the gun on consignment. I told him that I didn't, for the moment, and only wanted to know more about the revolver—how much it was worth, when and why this particular .357 had been made.

He cut in. "What it's made for is protection. What it's made for is save your damn life."

He handed back the gun. Slipping it into the canvas bag, I went into the daylight. Driving home, I could not shake the feeling that the men were standing at the counter running me down, Bass saying to Donny: "You believe that kid? Comes in to sell his grandfather's revolver."

And Donny, shaking his head: "Guy gets in a bad enough spot, he'll sell anything."

SEVERAL YEARS BEFORE THE trip to Bass's, I brought the revolver to another gun counter in a small Montana town. Of all the places I've been where a person can buy firearms, I liked that store best. It had a spacious, we've-got-what-you-need sensibility, like an old-time mercantile for hunters and fishermen. A tourist could walk through the front door dressed for Sunday brunch and leave equipped for a two-week elk hunt in the mountains, cast-iron skillet and all.

Perhaps a third of the store was devoted to guns, ammunition, and related paraphernalia, and I made my way there. It's strange entering a shop armed. I never got used to it and always expected an alarm to sound when I walked through the door.

For gun shop employees, an armed customer is normal. She might be there to sell an old shotgun, get something boresighted, or have a trigger adjusted. He might have a question about ammunition, as I did that afternoon when I walked in, nodded to the place's only other customer, and handed my .357 to the guy working the counter.

"What load," I asked, "would work best against a charging bear?" In those days, I spent a great deal of time on horseback and afoot on a high-mountain ranch. It was autumn, I had seen many grizzlies, and the prospect of being attacked was real.

"Three-fifty-seven's light for bear. You'd need to hit it good," the counterman said. He examined my revolver more closely, wrapped his fingers around the grips. "Better than nothing, though. Beautiful gun."

Walking to a rack of ammunition, he chose a box and brought it over.

"You need something solid. A bullet that'll penetrate."

Opening the box, he passed a cartridge to me.

"This is the heaviest that the three-fifty-seven will shoot," he said. "Heaviest I've got in the store, anyhow. Solid lead. Two hundred grains."

"*Shit*," said a voice behind me. "That won't do nothing but make a grizzly mad." The other customer—a bulky, bearded, pink-faced guy with a rumpled look—was threading his way through merchandise.

"You need this." He pointed to a huge silver semiautomatic pistol in the glass display case. "Take it out."

The counterman obliged, hauling up the pistol as if it were a big fish and setting it on the glass.

"Desert Eagle," the customer said, turning to me. "Fifty-caliber, bud. You been to Alaska? Big damn bears up there and this here is what they carry. Put a hole through a bear—I mean *through*—the size of a pie plate. One shot. *Bang*. Dead. Pile his ass up."

Ejecting the clip, he ran the slide and handed the weapon grip first to me. He had the sour reek of a big man who didn't look after himself—a smell somewhat like a bear that has been feeding on winterkill.

"*That* is a bear gun. For one thing, you can carry two clips and load it fast. That's a necessity. Goddamn necessity. Think a grizzly's gonna wait for you to put six bullets in that revolver?"

He looked at my .357. I found myself hoping he would not pick it up just as he reached out to do so, hefting it and sighting down the barrel, clicking the cylinder in and out with infuriating familiarity.

"What you got here, bud," he said, patting the .357 with his free hand, "ain't for bears. This's a *can* gun."

I stood at the counter, Desert Eagle in hand: *Tin can?* I wondered. *As in target practice? For shooting at cans?* He leaned forward, leering, rising onto the balls of his feet with the eager aspect of someone waiting for the other shoe to drop. *A joke,* I thought. *I didn't get it.*

There followed a silence during which the clerk wore a worried and slightly pleading look. His was an uncomplicated face: round features, short beard, wire glasses, a graying widow's peak above a pale forehead. He had been a long time behind the counter, grown old back there. Probably he had heard this all before.

"A *can* gun," the customer said, showing teeth. "Mexi-*cans*. Afri-*cans*. Indian Ameri-*cans*." He rapped the revolver's butt on the countertop to punctuate his list. "What you got is a *can* gun. Real pretty one, too."

Setting my revolver on the counter, the man was swiftly gone. He passed the rifle racks and boot displays on his way out of the shop's front door, where his exit made a small bell ring.

I stood there, mammoth pistol dangling at my side, like a bandit who had forgotten what he was about. For a handful of moments, I tried bending the meaning of his words toward anything but the ugly truth. It didn't work. He'd been clear. I knew what he had meant.

The clerk wore his same worried expression, now fixed on me. He did not speak.

"I don't want this," I said, handing him the Desert Eagle and tucking my revolver into its canvas sack. "I'll take the bullets, though."

YEARS ON, DRIVING HOME from Bass's Gun Rack, I turned north from Missoula on Highway 93 and climbed Evaro Hill. I passed the sign proclaiming, in Salish and English, the edge of the Flathead Indian Reservation, sovereign territory of the Confederated Salish, Kootenai, and Pend d'Oreille Tribes.

"*Can* gun" that man had said. "Indian Ameri*cans*." Time had passed, but his words stuck with me like dogshit in a lug-soled boot. I remembered his dirty-joke grin as he delivered the punch line. It bothered me then, and still does now, that I hadn't managed a retort.

It was the sort of moment when a quick-witted person might have engineered a reckoning, but I said nothing. My thoughts moved slowly. He said his piece, watched me long enough to ensure that the meaning landed, and split. It chafed me to recall him hustling out the door, moving spryly for a man of his girth, secure in the knowledge that he had gotten away with it. Driving on, coming nearer and nearer to the farm I called home, I grew surer with every mile that I would never sell the .357 while such men remained to buy it.

Shortly after that, while visiting my parents on Whidbey Island in Washington, I stood on a beach looking across Saratoga Passage toward Camano Head. Offshore, the bottom dropped out of Puget Sound, the seafloor plunging five hundred feet in a hundred yards.

That part of the sound is an underground canyon full of currents running one direction during ebb tide and another at flood, a place seldom and only briefly still. Once, I spent a whole summer of mornings fishing in midchannel. I'd wake up early and haul a plastic kayak downslope from the house my parents were building, heading for the water's edge. Slipping free of the shore, I'd pull for open water, trailing line and wishing for salmon.

I caught few fish but didn't mind. All that fishing summer, it was enough for me to paddle out before sunrise, trolling. Though that stretch of the sound is busy, I almost never had company at dawn. It was quiet and I coasted across the meniscus on water so black and cold that I never felt comfortable staring into it for long. Animals showed themselves: baitfish jumping, cormorants racing low across the water's surface, eagles hunting, a regular cohort of seals. Once, a gray whale rose twenty paces from me without warning, heaving past like a train passing through a station where it doesn't stop. With a huge explosive breath and the rushing sound of water, it was gone.

I stood on the shore, thinking that I might go out some early morning when the world was blue, through quicksilver water, my grandfather's gun in the bottom of the boat. At the channel's center, where dipping a hand is like reaching into Hades, I'd stop and wait as the kayak yawed through a circle.

Reaching out, I'd lower the revolver until the black Pacific closed around hand, cylinder, and barrel. There would be no noise when my fingers opened, just the sight of the gun tumbling away, diminishing, vanishing with a fish-belly flash.

It would be gone and I would paddle home unburdened. That would be its end, a final one. I knew what salt does to metal. Anything ferrous and unrinsed—a reel's arbor or the hardware on a kayak's bow—blooms rust and falls to pieces.

Years down the line, some fisherman might run deep for halibut, snag, and haul up a hunk of carbuncled metal. If he could recognize the thing, he'd ask why a gun was down there.

Pressed to answer that question, I'd say that the Smith & Wesson was in the depths because there are too many firearms up here on the surface. To look at a chart of per capita gun ownership by nation is to receive a lesson in American exceptionalism. There are more civilian-owned guns than human beings in this country. According to the Small Arms Survey, a nonprofit global tracking effort, there are 120 firearms for every 100 living, breathing humans in the United States, including babies and great-grandparents. No other nation comes close.

There are so many guns here that if our country finally descends into the kind of end-times street war that has become a too common fantasy, a lot of people will be shooting with both hands. Even without such a hideous general paroxysm, Americans do plenty of damage.

45,222: That, according to the Pew Research Center's analysis of statistics published by the Federal Bureau of Investigation and the Centers for Disease Control and Prevention, was the number of people killed by gunfire in the United States in 2020. Of those deaths—each one a real life's end with actual noise, blood, and grief—54 percent were suicide and 43 percent murder. The number of suicides—24,292 that year—strikes me particularly. It is terribly high. Though some of the total can be attributed to 2020's particular bleakness, the number follows a decades-long upward trend. If nothing else, the figures suggest that with so many guns at hand we cannot even trust ourselves.

The revolver wasn't with me when I stood on the beach looking at Puget Sound. Throwing it in the sea was only a thought. I did have the gun later that summer, though, when I climbed into the Mission Range, those egregiously vertical and grizzly-haunted peaks forming our farm's northern horizon, and picked my way through scree toward a snowfield. Not a glacier, though a few do persist in the Missions, but a city-block-size summer-grayed expanse of hardened snow at the base of a north-facing cliff. It was the kind of snow that never melts, growing only a bit smaller at the height of August. It was steep. Crossing it, working my way obliquely toward the upper edge, felt dangerous. To lose my feet meant sliding. A slide would not end well.

I kicked steps into the snow, ascending toward the water-streaked headwall, moving slowly, muscles burning. There, as expected, was the pit. Where deep snowpack meets stone, a void almost always forms. Rock warms with daylight even if it faces north. This fact, and the melting action of water running down from higher places and the downslope creep of so much frozen mass, creates a chasm.

German mountaineers, having named every possible convergence of rock and ice, call it *randkluft*—a marginal crevasse. The French say *rimaye*. Anyone, in whatever language, knows the yawning void as a place of no return.

Tugging my pack around, I took out my grandfather's gun. I studied the weapon, fixing its details in my mind, then glanced down the crevice to where the narrowing walls turned blue then black.

I could have opened my hand and let the revolver fall. Boulders would have ground it down and meltwater consumed its steel. It would have stayed under until the world warmed enough to make that snowfield fail.

I could have done it except for the fact that my grandfather would have loved the spot where I was standing. I was certain of it. He would have gloried in the serried mountains stretching northward. He'd have felt the place's gorgeous severity in his bones.

He loved Montana. Everyone in our family knew that. Most summers, whether he was living in Los Angeles or Seattle, he set out with his brother on road trips to Yellowstone and its surrounding valleys. He fished and sometimes hunted. He camped—initially in tents, then in a series of increasingly commodious trailers. Of the pictures I've seen, he looks happiest in the ones that were taken out here. In those photos, he's often dressed like a rancher in jeans, button-up shirts, and a brimmed hat. In the oldest photos, he looks like me.

I had the strangest feeling that he stood beside me looking across this beautiful rough country, loving it no less than my father loves the sea. It was that kinship, I suppose, and the unmistakable sense of having conjured him that made the gun seem precious and my course less clear.

To throw it away seemed a terrible waste. When it vanished into the dark, a part of my grandfather's memory would follow. Before I did what couldn't be undone, I decided, I ought to know him better. That is what I meant to do when I came out of the mountains.

PARENTS ARE NOT WHOLLY departed while their children draw breath. They cannot vanish while so many of their alleles, memories, stories, and possessions are kicking around the world. From my father, I learned that Robert Thorne Andrews had been born into a well-heeled family in Chicago, that he had been a sickly youth, and that his parents had moved west to Los Angeles for their son's health and certain business opportunities. A middling student, he left college for the Second World War. He never spoke of the war to my father except once. He'd traveled by commandeered train through ruined France, arriving in villages by night and sleeping in ditches, waking one morning to find himself

surrounded by the bloody rags and severed limbs of a field hospi-
tal. He was at the Battle of the Bulge and other of the European
theater's butcheries. Of actual fighting, he told one short story.

It happened in the last months of the war when the outcome
was generally known and the Allied armies were shoving the Nazis back into Germany. My grandfather was with the 137th In-
fantry by then, fighting in an antitank company that spent a lot of
time digging up landmines by hand.

On evening patrol duty, he and a small squad of men were
walking on one side of a country road, among fortifications, when
through the gloaming on the road's far side came an equal party
of Germans walking their own lines. The two groups could not
have missed each other, but no shots were fired. They didn't wave
or speak but simply passed in the twilight, all of them knowing
the war was nearly through, none wanting to die so late in it.

None of this helped decide things with the gun, but the story
about Nazis in the twilight made me think differently about my
grandfather. I pictured him as a young man with a rifle walking
that road and could not help wondering if the part of me that
shrunk from violence had been in him, too. The possibility of
such a thread running back through generations gave me a new
sense of relation. It turned my attention toward deeper roots.

On my mother's side, we are just a few generations removed
from Canadienne obscurity. Beyond Alphonsine and Nazaire
LaTraverse, ancestry is a murky ocean to our bunch. My grandmother, Constance Madeline Chartier, née Houle, assures us
that we are *French*—her emphasis, not mine. At Christmastime,
she cooks a meat stuffing with a name we cannot pronounce or
spell, which my mother accompanies with too much good cheese.
There is a rumor among my aunts that we descend from the fa-
mously virginal Joan of Arc. This suffices as a lineage.

On Dad's side, though, the generations are precisely recorded and stand within easier reach. His is one of those pedigreed old American families, with the paternal line particularly easy to follow.

Starting with my grandfather, I traced it back through generations of surgeons, bankers, businessmen, soldiers, and settlers until I ended up reading William Bradford's *Of Plymouth Plantation*. Bradford served as the Plymouth Colony's governor for decades and was my fourteenth great-grandfather. Opening that book, I found his account of landing in the New World.

> Being thus passed the vast ocean . . . they now had no friends to welcome them nor inns to entertain or refresh their weatherbeaten bodies; no houses or much less towns to repair to, to seek for succour. It is recorded in Scripture as a mercy to the Apostle and his shipwrecked company, that the barbarians showed them no small kindness in refreshing them, but these savage barbarians, when they met with them (as after will appear) were readier to fill their sides full of arrows than otherwise. And for the season it was winter, and they that know the winters of that country know them to be sharp and violent, and subject to cruel and fierce storms, dangerous to travel to known places, much more to search an unknown coast. Besides, what could they see but a hideous and desolate wilderness, full of beasts and wild men— and what multitudes there might be of them they knew not.

They knew not. It makes for a gripping family story: one hundred hungry, hapless, undersupplied religious fanatics dropped on the frigid New England shore. By spring, half were dead of disease. Starvation would have finished that work, had the Pilgrims not pillaged corn from a Nauset village nearby.

Reading that book, I was struck by the foolhardiness of the

project and the resilience, though not foresight, of the people who undertook it. There were moments when I felt a flickering pride. If nothing else, it seemed like great-etc.-grandfather William had gumption.

But there is another story, one so enormous and significant as to make Bradford's account of the colony read like the journal of a flea's life. The bug is active, even plucky. It jumps, bites, and increases itself. It is a brave and interesting little parasite, but after a while, the reader can't help wondering about the huge, warm, shifting skin on which the insect feeds and capers.

That other story, the bigger tale Bradford wrote without meaning to, is about the havoc wreaked upon the North American continent by European colonists, microbes, and weapons. That destruction is everywhere at the margins of the Pilgrims' world. It surrounded Plymouth Colony as entirely as any "hideous and desolate wilderness."

In that larger history, his people—my people—will steal land and water from every tribe they meet. They will shove aside or murder anyone who objects to assault and larceny on a continental scale. They will take fish and game with wanton frenzy, using ever more efficient tools, until the woods and streams are barren. They will invent or use the buffalo rifle, .357 Magnum, and .50-caliber Desert Eagle.

Given time, they will do unthinkable damage: plowing the oceanic expanse of the Great Plains, cutting nearly all the ancient forests, damming enough rivers to doom salmon runs that have endured since the Holocene's dawning. They will make pits of whole mountains and sully the sky.

His offspring—my ancestors—will not only wreak this havoc but learn to lionize the professional arts of ecological and cultural violence. They will love sodbusters, steel-driving men, loggers, and cowboys. They will fetishize the tools of such work.

This is particularly true of weapons like the one passed down to me. Such revolvers are enshrined as the "guns that won the West."

The "*can* gun" man, that loathsome customer, probably knows those words by heart. I suspect him of dreams in which he rides as savior, judge, and executioner through a savage land. In those fantasies, when a wild beast or man confronts him, he quick-draws from a holster.

One shot. *Bang*. Dead. The rider presses on. If part of him repents, he silences it. It was necessary, he tells his shrinking conscience. There was no other way.

Having ridden the horse, carried my grandfather's revolver, and stood as the tall unflinching white man in the panorama of American myths and dreams, I know something about what it means to "win the West." I want no further part in it.

From where I stand, I can see how much damage has been done. I can see back to the beginning, too, through the centuries to my fourteenth great-grandfather with Atlantic sand on his breeches, taking up a precious leaf of paper to write:

> Being thus arrived in a good harbor, and brought safe to land, they fell upon their knees and blessed the God of Heaven who had brought them over the vast and furious ocean and delivered them from all the perils and miseries thereof, again to set their feet on the firm and stable earth, their proper element.

Those lines suggest a man who was thankful, hardworking, and pious according to his lights. But this is just as true: His bunch came ashore with bullets. He was the spear tip, a plague flea, the first fusillade.

Centuries on, having chewed through the meat of a whole continent, fattening all the while, his descendants reached the Pacific. That was my grandfather's generation. There was nowhere else for them to go from California, no further West to find, and the Pilgrim sons and daughters were forced to choose: stare into the sunset, trying not to think too hard, or turn around and face the road that led them there.

When the revolver first came into my hands, I felt history vibrating in it. The weapon was alive with affinities. It shone with power. I thought that the leather cartridge belt around my waist tied me to a line of men who were strong, who endured and strove against a wilderness, who broke the world into shapes that pleased them. To carry that gun and be counted among such men was my inheritance as a settler's son.

For years, I embraced the bright side of that inheritance without looking much at its darkness. I have no excuse for this. My mother, the black-and-white photographer, taught me better. She taught me that only half of a thing's true shape is shown by reflected light. The other half is shadow. To illustrate this, she took me to look at Puget Sound. Stirred by a light wind, the water was a chaos of wavelets, each one of them half ink, half mercury. An artist's eye sees that negative space, she told me. It finds the dark places and the cracks.

She passed those secrets to me, expecting me to remember, but when I first saw the shining West, I forgot. I canonized people who carved hard livings from rough country, enshrined roping, herding, and breaking ground with big machines as noble labor, and considered Montana-born cowboys as a native aristocracy. I strove to emulate these Western scions, seldom looking critically at them or my chosen life.

But I am my mother's son, born with her eyes. Eventually, I developed doubts. They started small, as a suspicion that something was wrong with the way I treated livestock.

Every cow, studied closely, has her own way of being in the world. It's easy to ignore this while looking at two hundred head of Black Angus cattle, but the truth is that even a line-bred herd is made of individuals. Cows have preferences and affiliations. They nurture alliances and vendettas despite the fact that we have spent millennia nudging their species toward heft and dullness. Nature is incorrigible that way.

Most cowboys I worked with did not recognize this or weren't willing to discuss it beyond warning me when a bull was on the fight. They'd say "good mama" to a cow when she licked a newborn clean and stood quietly to suckle. Two days later, they'd cuss her as a "mean ol' rip" for menacing them when they came to tag and castrate her calf. Very seldom did they weigh the traits together and see the animal as she was. This willful blindness is unsurprising, because a modern large-scale stockman's work— raising livestock to be killed for strangers—is psychologically burdensome. It is easier to haul a load of calves to slaughter if you do not know one animal from another.

Looking away is meant to protect us, but it doesn't work. Instead, it precludes our learning from animals and comprehending the depth of our entwinement with them and the land. Absent this bond and knowledge, it is hard to avoid becoming lonesome, vengeful, and destructive. Much of this destruction is visited upon plants and soils.

By the time I began to think along these lines, I was experienced enough to recognize overgrazing, erosion, and ecological distress when I saw it. I saw it almost everywhere. The ground, once held in place and fertilized by the deep roots of native bunchgrasses, now raised a crop of Eurasian noxious weeds: spurge, hound's-tongue, knapweed. In many places, dirt had blown away, leaving the plants on earthen pedestals. Streambanks had fallen in, caving under hooves. These things were happening to greater extents on some ranches I knew and to lesser extents on others, but they were evident to some degree wherever I looked.

The overall impression that I got, and still get when I scan most of the pastures along any rural highway in Montana, is of increasing exhaustion. The land, which is capable of feeding people and perpetually renewing itself, has been worn down and out by our misuse.

There was something else: Many of the ranchers I worked with were as tired as their fields. They griped about the slim margins of their chosen or inherited work, the cost of fighting weeds and predators, and the rising price of diesel. They spoke like the best times had come and gone. The way they talked made clear that something within them was wearing thin, eroding with the soil.

Too many of them looked and acted like veterans of a long military campaign, soldiers kept too long in the field. It is no coincidence. For two hundred years, their way of life has been at war with the ecology of the American West. I do not mean this figuratively. A proper firefight has been going on since settlers crossed the plains.

On one side of the battle lines were the indigenous animals, plants, and peoples of the place we now call the West. On the other were herders, drovers, and sodbusters bent on clearing space in which they and their kept species might thrive. The settlers accomplished this with axes, plows, and bullets. Above all else, bullets. They shot

wolves, bears, and mountain lions until the big predators were ex-
terminated, or nearly so. They damaged Native communities and
states, wounding families and appropriating enormous tracts of land.

We live in a latter phase of this conflict and children study a version of its history in school. They learn something about the damage done to this continent and its Indigenous people. They should
know more of that hard history—the displacement of tribes, the
terrorization of civilizations, the wholesale theft of resources—and
be taught to respect and support the resilience of every enduring
Native culture.

We ought also to teach them how conquering the American
West marred the victorious colonists: That violence redounds
upon its authors, leaving them shamed, frustrated, alienated, and
ultimately homeless; that approaching the natural world as an en-
emy has echoed poisonously through generations; that we are now
suffering the consequences of a culture that chooses the gun as a
preeminent totem and tool.

On one ranch where I worked, I lived in a large and well-
appointed log house. Not long after settling in, I heard the story
of a foreman who had preceded me there. In the depths of winter,
under that same roof, he drank or dosed himself into the depths
of depression. Threatening suicide, he paced the kitchen with a
pistol in hand, back and forth past the oven where I would one
day cook. I never got all the details, but things were sorted out
over several hours without the worst happening. Maybe one of
the hired hands talked him down or the gun wasn't loaded. Having given two weeks of notice, the foreman drove his pickup truck
away toward another job, another herd, another combination of
dirty work and pretty sky, an unknown end.

His story weighed on me because it was like others I had heard,
some with uglier endings. Its shape was too familiar.

For a time, I thought I had discovered a malaise endemic to ranching. In fact, I had glimpsed the corner of something larger, a heartsickness that has become epidemic across the continent. I knew the sickness well enough, having suffered from it the winter after Salish died.

I could also see part of the malaise's cause. As a rancher, I had the privilege of saddling a horse and riding uphill into roadless, undiminished watersheds. Up there, I saw the landscape much as it had been before settlers, schemers, and the rest of us began tearing it to pieces. That was my advantage: I often stood far enough from the built-up, beaten-down modern West to view it in context.

Whenever I left the mountain pastures where I worked, I drove through valleys subdivided into twenty-acre parcels, each one the tiny fiefdom of a spec-built manor. When I headed to my nearest grocery city—Bozeman, Butte, or Missoula—I noticed exurban sprawl radiating outward like infection from a wound. Everywhere I traveled, wherever I looked, there were more buildings and less open land. There came a day when something clicked. I noticed a pattern of destruction everywhere around me.

We're getting it wrong in this beautiful, ravaged place. Not just ranchers, but every modern American still operating within the traditions and myths that brought us here. Over and over, we find a lovely valley, shoot it through the ecological heart, grind its bones to dust, and pour the foundation of an edifice less interesting than what existed before.

This approach was criminal when we turned it on tribal nations and their homelands. It was criminal when we rubbed out animals we classified as vermin. It remains criminal now, as we scalp prairies that overlay bitumen, gut mountains for their last rich veins, and subdivide fertile prairies that might otherwise sustain us.

For years, I couldn't understand why we kept at such work. I thought of our culture as a stumbling beast that caused accidental damage, like a blindfolded elephant. I could forgive an elephant for making a mess, though I'd like to catch the bastard who put the blindfold on.

I have become less charitable. Now, I refuse to accept the premise that we, individually or collectively, know not what we do. We know, for instance, that each generation since the coming of white settlers has left a diminished landscape to its children. We know that we are draining ancient aquifers at staggering rates and that we have converted most of the accessible metals and minerals into tailings ponds. We know that nearly all the ancient forest is gone and that our towns and cities are spreading in ways anathema to happiness.

For a long time, I wondered why we did all this. Now I understand and it terrifies me: We do it because we are lazy. We do it to stay comfortable. We do it because recent history is hard to look on. We do it because shuffling downhill to ecological and moral perdition is, for the moment, easier than facing an upward climb.

On the day I took the revolver down to Missoula to Bass's Gun Rack, I came home to the farm, stopped on the dirt road, and looked across our pastures. The .357 lay on the passenger-side floorboard, its outline visible through the canvas as if it were a patient under a sheet. Looking at it, I understood that the past was not a stone to be left by the roadside or a revolver to be thrown down a crevasse, from which I might walk away scot-free. The thing that I hoped to break with was braided into me, a violent inheritance strung through blood and bones. It lived in objects I kept and treasured, like my grandfather's gun. In such cases, change is not a matter of wanting but of work.

Not long ago, I jogged up a forest trail behind our farm into the steep mountains. The land, which belongs to the Confederated Salish and Kootenai Tribes, remains untamed: miles of brushy logging roads and deer trails; pines, larches, and undergrowth; many carnivores. Upslope half a mile from my daily loop, the South Fork Jocko Tribal Primitive Area begins. Only tribal members can enter and they usually choose easier routes than the stony, overgrown course of Agency Creek. As a result, the forest sees little human traffic.

I followed a game trail to where the two forks of Agency Creek converge. Along the banks are light-starved spruces, ancient ponderosas, and a scattering of many-trunked birch trees caught in the act of simultaneously growing fast and falling down. The ground is boggy and uneven, scattered with boulders. In springtime, clear water rises in the swales.

Maybe you've seen this place—the kind of grown-over bottomland that brings grizzlies to mind, where people feel safer with a weapon. I slowed to a walk in there out of respect for the spot's affinities and because I did not want to sprain an ankle.

Past Agency Creek, the trail diminished. Stretches were clear only to the height of a deer's back and I had to go on all fours. The creek was beautiful, with sun raying through trees and the moss vividly green. It was windless and silent except for the sound of water. My heeler pup sprinted loops, rushed me, and shot off in the grip of ecstasy.

Emerging onto a logging road, I ran again. I heard an engine somewhere up the track and stepped into the brush to let the vehicle pass.

It came fast, an ATV throwing dust. The driver did not see me until we were quite near each other. Crouching to keep hold of the young dog's collar, I must have been half hidden in the bushes. Perhaps I was not immediately recognizable as human.

The driver startled and swerved. He was a thin man, dressed in Wrangler jeans and a button-up shirt. His pale narrow face tracked me as we came abreast. In what felt like slow motion, his hand moved to the handle of a pistol on his hip.

I raised my arm in greeting or surrender—would have raised both if not for the dog—proving at least that I was not a lion, bigfoot, or bear. He relaxed, gun hand rising in salute. Revving the engine, he was swiftly gone.

The pup whined, and my heart racketed. I stood as the noise and exhaust dissipated. For a moment, I had been a dangerous wild thing in his eyes. A hard and unforgettable expression had crossed his face as he had reached for the gun. Fear was most of it, but there was also a sneering challenge.

Whatever you are, *that look said,* I'll pull the trigger. *He'd fell me in the wayside brush and clatter onward through the mountains.*

Farther down the two-track road, I paused at a high place where I could look across the Jocko Valley. I stood panting, studying gridded roads and fence lines, clustered houses, dark knots of cattle in my neighbors' fields. I heard the distant constant noise of traffic on Highway 93. Fifteen thousand cars, someone had told me, on an average busy day.

The man's hard expression returned to me. I considered his slitted blue eyes, the tight line of his lips, that aspect of grim determination.

He had turned and put his hand on the gun. I had showed my pale open palm in surrender. In the instant before that hand was up, I saw that he was dangerous and afraid, and that his strength lived in the pistol. He was indignant that the forest had set a trap for him, but he was unsurprised. There was his weapon at the ready. He had come prepared to fight a wilderness, wearing the killing look that settlers have aimed at this place and its people for two hundred years.

Except for small birds moving in the canopy, the forest was still. In time, a clear thought came into my mind: I am not like him. I repeated those words until they were a declaration, until I was nearly convinced. I am not like that man anymore. Not since I learned to look differently at mountains.

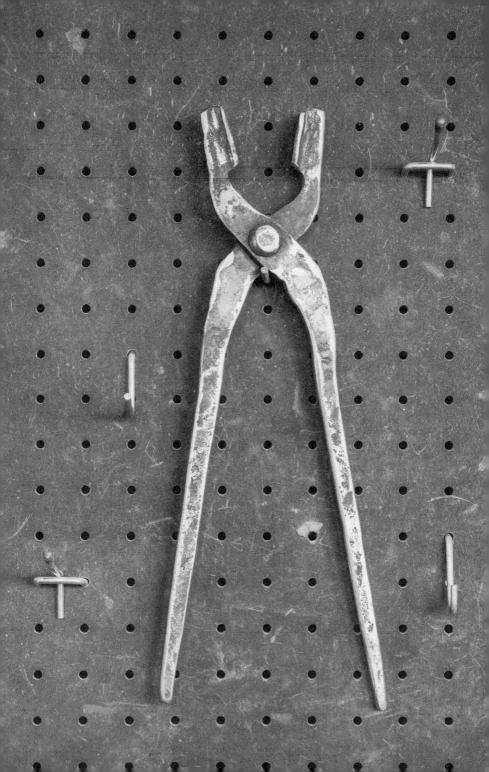

8

HAMMER AND TONGS

I FANTASIZED ABOUT DESTROYING my grandfather's gun. One day I considered bisecting the thing with a hacksaw, the next I imagined throwing it into a volcano. I did away with the revolver a hundred times in my mind but never took action. To simply break it or toss it away seemed a disrespectful waste.

An idea came to me: *Make it into something else.* It was a fine notion, but I knew nothing about metalworking. I sent off for several books and soon understood that it would be best to reshape the gun by forging rather than melting it down. Steel, if liquified in a furnace, must be handled expertly to retain its strength and malleability. Lacking experience and equipment of any kind, I decided that an anvil and hammer rather than a crucible were my best chance at remaking my grandfather's gift as a useful tool.

I found an old coal forge in a neighbor's barn and offered seventy dollars. The contraption did not look promising. Hadn't run in decades, the neighbor warned me. Not since the death of his grandfather, who had bought the cast-iron fire pan, welded on legs and steel wheels, and hooked up an electric motor to the blower with pulleys and belts.

My neighbor pocketed the money and helped to hoist the thing into my truck. "Good luck," he said.

Forges come in endless shapes and sizes, from industrial giants that swallow telephone-pole-size billets to knife-making ovens no bigger than a shoebox. Mine fell somewhere in the middle; its fire pan was the size and shape of a bassinet. At the pan's center was a funnel-shaped depression, with the blower's outlet at bottom. It was the kind of forge that would have been indispensable on farms and ranches until recently, perfect for shaping horseshoes and straightening plow shanks.

The thing was painted a faded red that had worn or baked away to bare metal in places. One of the legs was rusted through. I used the tractor bucket to unload it, wheeling it carefully into the farm's three-walled machine shed.

Dislodging pack rat nests from between the blower's fan blades, I greased every hub and bearing I could find. I spun flywheels and pulleys until they stopped grinding and moved with an easy hiss.

When I flipped the scavenged light switch that I assumed would turn the thing on, there followed several seconds of strained electric buzzing and the smell of a frying dynamo. As I reached to shut the switch off, the forge coughed dust and groaned to life.

Once the motor broke free, it ran with a pleasant thrum. The forge was one of those lovely, naked, belt-driven machines that have grown rare in the electronic age. Its mechanism was simple: a motor turned a shaft, the shaft ran a drive belt, and the belt spun the blades of a blower that brought cold musty air howling up from the firepot.

It blew hard. When I built a small test fire, the forge spat flaming newspaper and kindling across the shed. Pleased with the thing's strength, I ran back and forth stamping embers.

After a handful of attempts, I learned that tugging a crude lever at one end of the fire pan brought the drive belt into contact with the blower's flywheel. When I got the tension right, anything in the bowl burned fast and hot, vanishing in gouts of white flame. At first, I tried to use wood. Filling the furnace bowl with the scrap ends of two-by-fours, I applied spark and air, and set a bit of rebar atop the conflagration. Flames leapt up and heat came off in waves, but even after several minutes, the metal did nothing more than turn a sullen red. When I pulled it out and struck a blow, the hammer hardly left a mark.

I fetched a bag of charcoal from beside the barbeque and tried again. The briquettes melted like ice cubes, half their blackened sawdust flaring into smoke, the other half blowing off unburned to settle on every surface around.

I threw in briquettes by the handful until the rebar turned orange and glowed brighter than before. I pulled it from the fire with a pair of vise grips. The metal flattened when I hammered it against a makeshift anvil. I managed two rounds of this before the charcoal was gone, ending up with something shaped like a flattened outsize golf tee.

With more pride than was warranted, I brought the thing indoors to show Gillian.

"Look in the mirror," she said. A miner—white-eyed, soot-skinned—grinned back.

In short order, I came to understand that I needed coal. It was not easily come by in my part of the world. There was irony in this, since a mile-long five-engine train of the stuff rolled daily through Missoula en route from the Powder River Basin to port cities on the Pacific. At the railyard, I could stand behind a chain-link fence and watch black-heaped 120-ton carloads passing in an endless clatter but could not get my hands on a fifty-pound sack.

When I finally found a source of good bituminous coal, I learned quickly that there was an art to burning it. I had to build fires slowly, working from smaller to larger chunks, feeding the blaze from a wetted heap around the firepot.

When things were right, the flame burned white and clean. If something was off, a plume of green-black smoke billowed up. It was an ugly, toxic cloud. Gillian checked often to see whether the shed had caught fire.

Still, I was forging, experimenting on all manner of farm scraps. I scavenged a big piece of hardened steel to use as an anvil, fixing it atop a thick wooden pedestal. Gillian gave me several old hammers as a gift.

Once I understood how to operate my forge, I taught myself how to shape and move metal. The most basic techniques are bending, upsetting, and drawing out. Bending is the easiest: Wait until the metal is hot enough, hang it over the side of something solid, start swinging. Adding a twist is simple, too, if the smith has a vice and tongs.

Upsetting and drawing out take more practice. The former is the act of thickening heated stock with endwise hammer blows. Done well, it creates a pregnant bulge or a knob that can become a bolt end. Drawing out is the opposite process—thinning and lengthening a piece of metal with well-aimed hammering. A pitchfork's tines, for example, have been drawn out into points.

I practiced these operations with mixed results, making coat hooks and pot hangers using several patterns. Nothing about the work was healthy. Each day I emerged smirched, with a racking cough, black-ringed nostrils, and a feeling of having been charbroiled inside and out. The smoke was particularly hard on my eyes, which stung, reddened, and sometimes forced themselves shut.

Often, in the course of working a piece of metal, I had occasion to wonder if I had become a weakling or was swinging my hammer wrong. My projects progressed slowly, requiring many trips between anvil and fire—many heats. Once, I tried to shape a small leaf from a half-inch rod. It took an hour and the tired metal shattered in the end.

There was magic in forging steel, but I had seldom seen a process so clearly and directly pollute the sky. Day after day, I fed the firepot's hungry mouth and smoke billowed up. I burned fifty pounds of coal in my first two weeks of forging, releasing about the same amount of carbon dioxide as a tree combs from the air in a year.

Sometimes, after putting in hours at the forge, I'd come indoors with my face so filthy that Gillian would not kiss me. Then I would walk down to the basement and study the revolver, examining its absolute precision: how hammer and trigger danced together, how the cylinder spun soundlessly on its axis. I would marvel at the smoothness of the action and wonder if tomorrow would be the day that I took the beautiful lethal machine to the shed and threw it into the fire.

When I held one of my creations beside the revolver, the contrast dismayed me. My forge projects were rough, to put things charitably. I could manage simple shapes—a hook, a heart bent and joined at the bottom, a poker—but no matter how hard I tried, I could not make anything nearly as useful or beautiful as that gun.

In such moments, I couldn't stand the idea of lifting a hammer above the revolver and swinging with all my strength. It seemed like trading more for less, like vandalism. I am not, by my nature, a vandal. I resolved to practice until I could do justice to the Smith & Wesson.

Around that time, after dark on a winter night, a neighbor called to warn us that a man was walking up our county gravel road dressed in black and firing a gun.

"At people?" I asked.

She knew no details, only that somebody was out there shooting. "Pull your curtains and lock your doors," she said, half joking, but with an edge to her voice. "Hide under the bed!"

We had no curtains, being far from other houses. Our living room was a lit fishbowl, our blindness perfect, with each windowpane a flat black plane and all sound muffled by the new insulation I had spent the summer installing.

Suddenly, almost on our doorstep—we were one of the last houses on the road the shooter was walking on—was the terror of our age. I was afraid and could imagine the look of our home from without. I could see the two of us at our kitchen table, silhouetted like targets at a range.

A disgruntled, broken person with a weapon in hand. A desperate man. To think of him dredges up stories that I would prefer to forget, like the one about the guy who rode a bus from several states away, hitchhiked up a nearby valley, walked miles down a dirt road to a solitary house, and out of pure random malice or lunacy murdered the couple who lived there. He did not know them from Adam. He did not know where he was. Still, he killed.

I relayed the news to Gillian and called the sheriff's office. The dispatcher had no information at all. A deputy would head our way from town. She told us to wait indoors.

Locking the doors, I went to the back room for my grandfather's gun. I filled the revolver with the heavy bullets I used when grizzly bears were around. Usually, I loaded five rounds then spun the cylinder so an empty chamber sat below the gun's hammer and firing pin. I did this because I worried about cartridges going off spontaneously—a thing gun nuts tell me is so vanishingly unlikely as to be impossible—or that something might bump the revolver's hammer. That night, though, I loaded the revolver completely. Gillian watched me come upstairs with the holster in hand. She surprised me with a glance of approval.

I wondered where to put the thing. Hanging the cartridge belt from our bedpost struck me as too ostentatiously Western. Under the bed wouldn't do. Sometimes our friends visit with children. Settling finally on the closet's top shelf, I curled the belt around the holster, made double sure the hammer wasn't cocked, and left the gun there.

The morning after, we woke to a crisp, bright dawn. It was hard to remember fear. I forgot about the gun for several days. Snow kept falling, inches making feet, with a hard wind now and again sculpting drifts that closed our road.

Early one morning, I went out to start the tractor warming. It was the blue hunting hour. Coming back from the shop, I could see deer clustered near a hayshed in our back field.

I came up the half landing from the front door, gained our living room, and stopped in my tracks. It was as if the bedroom wall had vanished and I stared straight down the revolver's barrel. I could see bullet noses in chambers; the firing pin's point; the swirl of rifling; the front site's small gnomon, the open mouth. I could see cold death in my own closet, head high, aimed my way.

Sometimes, I wanted to be rid of the revolver immediately and forever. Sometimes, as on the evening when the gunman walked our road, I couldn't imagine being without the weapon's protection.

I kept blacksmithing, spending as much time as I could with a hammer in hand. Soon, though, I reached a plateau: I could bend, twist, and flatten hot metal. I could make passable coat hooks, but none of my crude techniques seemed worthy of my grandfather's gun. I still knew little about what the gun's steel could do. I wondered if it could ever become a serviceable axe head. If the barrel, frame, and cylinder could be flattened into a shovel that wouldn't shatter. In time, I realized that I'd need to learn these things from someone. That's why I called Dan'l Moore, the father of one of Gillian's oldest friends.

Broad-shouldered, laconic, and easygoing, he was precisely the sort of man I expected to find beside a forge. Dan'l—*A fine name for a smith*, I thought—made beautiful wrought iron, hinges, and hardware in his shop. He was kind enough to spend two days showing me how to swing a hammer efficiently, a thing requiring more technique than I had imagined.

Dan'l put me to a series of exercises: making round stock square and square stock round, drawing out billets into tapered points, spreading and curling the ends of steel scraps. He demonstrated each step of the process with brief good-natured instructions. I was struck by the steady rhythm of his work, the way hammer strokes became a drumbeat. He moved the workpiece deftly, flipping red-hot metal one way then the other so the blows pushed and tapered steel just as he wanted them to.

That is the mesmerizing thing about a proficient smith: The hammering half of him or her is a machine, its movements powerful and predictable. *Whack . . . whack . . . whack,* and so on until the job is done. The other half of the smith's body moves like a feeding bird. That hand darts and flicks, perpetually adjusting, turning the tongs one way and another, drawing hot metal across the anvil's face or positioning it to be bent around the tapered horn.

I watched Dan'l closely and tried to imitate his movements. It was difficult, like learning to play guitar. No sooner did I focus on one hand's task than the other went haywire.

We made a set of smith's tongs together. It was far and away the most complicated thing I'd created from metal and I was proud of the result. When we finished, I set my project on a steel workbench and watched it fade to black.

We stood in the shop drinking beer, looking at a photo album. He had made carriage lanterns and decorative chests, staircases and bells, all manner of latches, racks, and hangers. These things impressed me, but my eyes kept shifting to the cooling tongs.

It pleased and surprised me to have made a functional tool, to have fashioned something that held the potential of further creation. That was the great wonder of forging: A smith could make a hammer. That hammer could shape a plow, a shovel, a sword, or a thousand other useful things. With time, material, and fuel, a metalworker could rebuild the industrial age from scratch.

I said as much to Dan'l, who went on flipping the album's plastic pages.

"Could build most of it," he said. "With the right metal. Take a while, though."

"How about the revolver?" I said. He knew something of my intentions. "Could I turn it into something useable? An axe, a knife, or something?"

"Maybe," he said. "Depends what the steel is, what equipment you have to work with, and how good you get with a hammer. Tell you one thing—it'll be harder than making tongs. You'd be forge welding to take all that air space out of the frame and barrel, just to get a solid piece of metal to work with. You'd need the heat just right. Need to get everything right, and you'd only get one shot."

"We could do it here," he said. "Maybe. But if you really want to end up with a tool you can use, you should look up Jeffrey Funk."

After Dan'l said this, I heard rumors of Jeffrey Funk everywhere. Another Flathead Valley blacksmith recommended him, adding that Funk's workshop was a wonderland. A person could make anything there. If a thing could be done with steel, it could happen under Jeffrey's roof.

The man's reputation had reached as far as the West Coast. My father told me about a conversation he'd had with a neighbor on Whidbey Island. The neighbor had a penchant for accumulating things. He had a collection of anvils and related paraphernalia, which my father had either seen or heard of. Out on the road between their houses, my dad got talking about my newfound interest in hammers and fire. The neighbor listened, nodding.

"Where's your son living again?"

My father told him.

"The best blacksmith in the country is in western Montana," the neighbor said. "His name is Jeffrey Funk."

Then came a dinner with some young farmers up in the Mission Valley. One of the hosts, like me, was learning to work metal. He showed me his small gas forge and several pieces of pretty hardware.

"I'm still learning," he said. "There's a blacksmithing school up near Kalispell, and if I ever get a couple weeks free, I'm going up. You know about Funk, right?"

For a period of weeks in early spring, it seemed like I couldn't turn a corner without running into some trace of Jeffrey the toolmaker, master smith, teacher, guru. He would have been easy enough to track down, but I didn't pick up the phone. I still did not know precisely what I'd be asking him to help me make.

Afternoons, when my work was done, I'd leave the farm by the uppermost gate, passing from pastureland into forest. I'd walk in the trees, wondering: *Something for the farm? Pitchfork? Pickaxe? A hammer?*

At that season, I almost always saw black bears when I walked or ran in the woods. I learned to recognize them in brush: shoulders and ears, deft slow shuffle. I learned the black bear's name in Salish, n̓ɫámqeʔ, and said it when I met a boar or sow on the logging roads. My neighbor recommended that. He said that only white people had trouble with bears and that it helped to call animals by their proper names. His family had been greeting n̓ɫámqeʔ and smx̣éy̓č'n—grizzly—for thousands of years. My pronunciation was imperfect, but I took his advice. N̓ɫámqeʔ, I'd say. X̣est sx̣lx̣alt. "Good day, black bear."

One rain-soaked morning as a storm rolled northeast, I trotted up a faint trail beginning at Agency Creek. Looking uphill as I rounded a corner, I saw a brown trundling rump. Black bear or grizzly, I couldn't say, though the former was more likely in those woods. It was a big, close, healthy, chestnut-colored bear. I stopped in my tracks, heart hammering so loudly that the creature could have heard it.

The next morning, I went again through cow pastures and over a wooden brace in our uppermost fence into the forest. That area, a patch of private ground between our place and tribal land, is grown over with hawthorn, mountain maple, and chokecherry to a height of about fifteen feet. Old pines erupt from the understory.

The grove, which Gillian and I call the Triangle, is a wild place with no good way through its heart. The nearest easy path is a disused two-track road along an earthen irrigation canal. Those ruts skirt the Triangle's edge but never enter.

Following that nominal road, I looked left and saw something large and dark in the greenery. Yesterday's bear. His color was the same dark brown. The cockleburs on his haunches looked familiar.

He rose to his hind legs, swaying, his upper half visible. He was a black bear, full-grown and in good health, with a white chevron blaze on his chest. I say "he" because I believed he was a boar. No cubs were with him and he had a masculine thick-necked square-headedness.

He stood huffing air, forelegs dangling. We were close, separated by ten paces of low brush. For a moment, all was still. It was only when I took a backward step along the path that he moved, too, dropping onto all fours, turning away. With a long smooth stride, he vanished into a wall of growth. I heard rustling for a moment then, from the thicket's heart, the chatter of discomfited birds.

I've seen many bears, but this one fascinated me. I supposed that he lived in the knot of trees above my farm, a thing that struck me because of how small the thicket was—no more than fifty yards across at the widest—and how close it stood to the working lands of the valley floor. I drove tractors through the fields below that grove. I herded cattle and irrigated there, and walked about chopping thistles. The bear, if he called those trees home, was our nearest neighbor.

Retreating a little, I sat on a huge old burned-out ponderosa stump in our high pasture and kept watch on the dark line of the timber. The bear did not emerge.

All that day, when I looked uphill from the living-room window or paused in the fields, I'd study the Triangle's edge intently. I didn't expect to see the bear in broad daylight, but I believed that he was there.

In the late afternoon, I took two motion-activated trail cameras to the place where I had seen him enter the thicket and stood listening. Birds kept up their usual talk. Irrigation water gurgled in the canal.

"Ṉɫámqeʔ," I said after a while. "I'm coming in."

Starting down the game trail, I maintained a halting flow of talk. The birds went quiet and the sound of ditchwater faded as I came to where the bear had stood earlier. Ahead, the hawthorns formed a waist-high tunnel into which the path disappeared. Farther in, rising above everything else, was the trunk of a solitary ponderosa. It was an immense ancient thing, predating cattle, farmers, the timber industry, firearms.

To follow the trail meant going to ground. I set my hands against the moist black soil and crawled. Two feet on, I felt a sudden pain. Lifting my hand, I found a twig pinned to my flesh with inch-long hawthorn spines. That thicket held the Jocko Valley's full rogues' gallery of spiked plants—Woods' roses, teasel, nettles, and several varieties of thistle. For a while, I forgot the bear and thought only of my hands and knees.

Coming to a small open place at the huge tree's base, I found what I was after. Several game trails converged there, each departing in its own direction. The ground had been beaten flat with use, littered everywhere with scat. A shallow ovoid depression had been scraped in the needle duff between the roots. I hung my cameras on the trunk of a smaller pine, set them to record video, and left the way I'd come.

I waited two weeks before going back—again announcing myself at the thicket's edge, again picking my way through spinous defenses. When I made it home and connected the cameras to my computer, the risk and perforations seemed worthwhile. Bears appeared on camera almost every day—not just the white-blazed boar but several others. They visited in turn, mostly at night, coming along paths from the mountains or valley, loitering near the tree before passing out of frame. They moved carefully, each picking its way. None of them liked walking on hawthorn branches.

One yearling had pressed its nose so close that the camera lens fogged over. Quite gently, it took the camera into its mouth. The frame shook and went black. The image returned after a few seconds, its field of view tilted downward and hazed by saliva.

Bears were not the only animals. There were bobcats and coyotes, owls and eagles. A few hours after the passage of several wary deer, a mountain lion slid through the frame. It moved with an unmistakable languid power, spreading each forepaw before setting it down.

I've always been afraid of mountain lions—more so than of the other big carnivores—because they make such an art of stealth. The beast on my camera floated like a ghost. Its tail caressed the air seemingly with a life and mind of its own. Though I've found tracks enough to know that I share the mountains with several big cats, I've only once had occasion to greet a mountain lion—skʷtismyé—by name. There have been other close brushes, I am sure.

It seemed that every wild creature, large or small, made use of the Triangle's thick-grown timber. There were badgers, snakes, and uncountable songbirds. There were hawks and vultures, chipmunks and voles. From the cameras and my other visits, I came to understand that the stand of trees above our southeast corner, nearly impassable to us, was as crowded with wild animals as it was overgrown with plants. I've seen wolf tracks running through. I've found moose and elk sign. Stacy Courville, a friend of mine and the carnivore biologist for the Confederated Salish and Kootenai Tribes, showed me GPS collar data that put grizzlies there.

Later that day, I was out in the shop hammering a piece of scrap steel into yet another coat hook, thinking about the Triangle. Not all the forest around here is so brimming with life. That grove is special because it sits at the edge of the valley floor and its soil holds enough water to foster dense growth. It is a last redoubt of cover for animals preparing to brave the open ranching country.

The Triangle was particularly valuable to wild things, I realized, because of where it lay in the landscape.

For the same reason, the Jocko is of crucial importance to western Montana's ecology. Our small valley matters because it is the southern extremity of the Northern Continental Divide Ecosystem—a vertebral column of peaks reaching north to the Yukon and interrupted only by a handful of roads. The curling tailbone of that rocky spine wraps partway around our farm, forming the valley's southern rim.

Nature moves freely in those mountains without regard for national boundaries, reservations, or property lines. If the animals go much farther south than our place, though, the untrammeled country peters out, giving way to Missoula's sprawl and the busy corridor of Interstate 90. Other ranges lie in that direction—the Selway-Bitterroot and the Frank Church–River of No Return Wildernesses, which together comprise the largest roadless area remaining in the Lower 48—but reaching them requires a south and westward journey across the Jocko Valley's floor.

Because the valley is full of farms, livestock, and houses, the crossing is difficult and often dangerous for wildlife. Perhaps the best proof of this is the fact that grizzlies are common on our side of the Jocko, but when a collared sow or boar goes more than a dozen miles southwest of here, avoids being shot for eating sheep or chickens, and crosses Interstate 90, it makes the news.

I paused my work. The metal in my tongs had gone black, but a fierce heat burned from it as I walked to the shop's open side. To my north and east were steep forested mountains. South and west, the land was fenced and plowed.

It struck me that I lived in the narrow part of a bottleneck, a place wild things had to pass through as they sought out good habitat, mates, and food. Some creatures were managing the crossing already. The farm had its share of bears and deer in summer and autumn. But I had watched those animals, particularly the bruins, for several years. They came at night to try their luck and never seemed comfortable in open fields. Many of them had been shot at and were not fools. Daylight sent them back toward the Triangle at a lope, glancing back to see if anyone had given chase or lobbed a bullet at their straining haunches.

What would it take for such animals—not only bears but the rest of nature's throng—to move more easily across the Jocko? They needed sheltering groves like the Triangle scattered like stepping-stones across the valley floor. They needed thickets to rest, feed, and hide in to avoid what we've done to most of their world.

A few old ponderosas grow in our highest pasture, forming a rough line pointing downhill from the mountains toward our Quonset hayshed. Cattle loaf and seek shade at the base of these trees in summertime and eagles roost in the branches.

There used to be forest here, I thought. Not everywhere on the farm but in places. The big pines and relic stumps proved it. Wild animals seemed to remember. Not so long ago, timber had licked partway out across the fields.

For weeks, I had been hearing the words "swords into plowshares." "Beating swords into plowshares," or some version thereof, was what people often said when I talked about the idea of forging my grandfather's revolver into something else. I never liked that saying. In an essential way, it seemed at odds with what I meant to do with the revolver.

Looking across cleared land to the dark-timbered mountains, I had no interest in making a plowshare. A plow, after all, is another kind of sword. Like the gun my grandfather passed to me, it is one of the tools that brought us to where we are in the West.

I did not want a plow, an axe, or any other implement designed to carve up wilderness or turn a whole field's sod upside down. Instead, I wanted something that would help me bring an older, wilder world back into being.

AROUND THE SAME TIME I made that decision, I drove an hour and a half north from the farm to read from a book I had written about grizzly bears. It was a small-town event, held in a brewery and organized by a local nonprofit group, but there was a large crowd. Nothing in my agricultural life, not picking field-stone, setting fence posts, or loading angry bulls into trailers, wears me out as much as giving such talks. At the end of such an evening, I feel like a spent battery. More than once, I've gone straight to the parking lot, crawled into the cab of my pickup truck, and passed out.

That night in Bigfork, I talked about grizzly conservation and told stories. I tried to convey certain things: how we stood at a crucial moment in our regional history with the great bear; how our actions over the next two or three decades would either pre-serve or destroy countless animals and ecosystems; that we gain something real, if difficult to measure, from sharing the landscape with grizzlies.

After the questions and answers, I stood on the little stage gathering papers from the podium, hoping I could keep awake on the drive home. Looking up from stowing my things, I saw a man walking my way through the departing crowd. He was around my father's age, with a mane of unruly, mostly white hair emerging from a brimless cloth cap. Small and wiry, he moved through the crowd with unmistakable energy and the forward cant of a person leaning into wind. As he neared, I saw a curve in his shoulders that I have come to recognize as the mark of a working life.

"The world needs a lot more people like you," he said without preamble.

From that beginning, which is a fine way to greet anyone, he told me that he lived outside Bigfork near the base of the Swan Range and saw black bears on his property frequently. He asked what I knew about grizzlies moving back into his part of the Flathead Valley. He listened to my answer closely, nodding.

"Doesn't bother me," he said, looking genuinely pleased at the thought of grizzlies crossing his land; and he launched into the story of a bear encounter in the higher mountains. There was something compelling in his way of speaking. He gathered momentum, hurrying toward some crucial fact or moment, talking faster and more energetically, then halting to judge his words' effect on me. He had thin, puckish features, a nose that curved to one side as if it had been broken long ago, and intent blue eyes.

He stuck his right hand, a thick-knuckled, callused mitt that seemed a full size too big for his arm, into the space between us.

"Jeffery Funk," he said. "Nice to meet you."

The Jocko Agency was built in 1862 half a mile downhill from the land that is now our farm. That's how the creek behind our place got the name it carries now and how part of the valley came to be called "Where They Distribute Things" in Salish. What the creek was named before, I've not yet learned. The Jocko Agency's original storehouse and quarters are long gone, but a small white church and a cemetery remain on the site. The church no longer holds services, so far as I can tell, but the graveyard gets used. Recently, a tribal elder was buried there.

I was cleaning the irrigation ditch, hauling a winter's worth of fallen limbs clear of the channel on a fine cold morning. The grass was short and green. Small white clouds sailed over. For some minutes, the wind kept me from understanding that the faint sound I heard was, in fact, many people singing. The graveyard was distant, the branches of the ditch-bank cottonwoods whistled as gusts moved through, and the song rose and fell elusively. I stopped working several times but could not hear it well.

Setting aside my task, I walked down through the hayfield to the corner where our land meets the county road. From there, I could distinguish the rhythm of drumming and the harmonies of several voices. I made out many cars in the graveyard and a large group of people standing in a semicircle.

The melody had an aching, airy rise and fall. A musician would know better how to describe what I heard and why it lifted my spirit and struck at my heart all at once. A fluent speaker of Salish could have told me what the song meant. Because I am neither, I could only listen.

I did not want to pry or be a tourist at anyone's funeral. I stayed on the county road a quarter mile from the cemetery. I heard the beauty of that song, in which one voice rose above the others, keening in a language I couldn't understand. The sound of the drum was round and hollow, and seemed to fill the world.

There were hawks in the air. There are almost always hawks here, but that day there were many. Two, then four, then six redtails coasted southwest up the wind. They came from the wild apron of the Mission Range, descending with set wings until they were straight overhead then pinwheeling upward in spirals. They looked down on our farm, the graveyard, and the road, calling to one another through the clear sky.

I listened to the honor song and hawk cries mixing. The birds circled for a long time, always higher. To my ears, the languages had a certain resemblance. Both, at least, evoked grief and solace.

If a people live in a landscape long enough and pay close attention, it makes sense that one of their burial songs should sound a bit like the crying of hawks. For how many generations, I wondered as I walked home, must people sing that song before birds, prodigious mimics that they are, recognize the refrains? Does a thousand years suffice for such convergence? Ten thousand? I found it hard to think in such numbers. The Salish have lived longer than that in these valleys.

Going back up the road, the sound growing fainter, I was gripped by a strange jealousy for the dead man and the people sending him on. I wanted to be buried that way: ringed by members of my tribe, overflown by hawks, laid to rest in a soil my people have belonged to since time immemorial. But that is not my lot.

For the first time in my life, I understood that it is lonely to be alive without a tribe. I have a family, but that's not the same. We are scattered to the winds, joined by blood but having few sustaining traditions, claiming hometowns and homelands only temporarily, tenuously. Movement is our constant: over the ocean from Europe, across the wide North American continent. For generations, we have believed that we belong nowhere except west of where we happened to be born. With a host of other colonial clans, we swarmed into the sunset, taking little notice of what we trampled underfoot or the people displaced by our coming.

Something about that morning—the singing, the people by the graveside, that depth of history in one place—cast my own family's rootlessness into sharp relief. It made me think that my forebears had missed the point of something profound, becoming blind and deaf to an essential part of what a human life should be. It made me think that we were lost and had been for a while.

Years ago, Gillian and I followed a jaguar researcher on his rounds through a remote Central American jungle. Having macheted through miles of vines while sweating buckets, we came to a place on the seashore where thousands of Urania moths poured north to south above our heads in a continuous throng.

The black and iridescent green *Urania* is wider across its out-spread wings than a man's palm.

Each heart-shaped insect was striking enough that, had I seen it singly in a garden, I'd have stopped in wonder. On that beach, they were countless, flowing overhead in a river of wings and color on an annual migration that took several weeks to pass each waypoint along the coast. They flew over, beating. Our world felt changed because of seeing them.

My Salish neighbors' honor song was like that. Everything seemed different with the melody in the air. I was sensible to its beauty and, to some degree, its history, but I knew I stood apart. They sang in harmony. I listened at a distance, alone.

Just then, it seemed a shame to go through life knowing that I wouldn't be buried with a song refined over millennia to match these mountains, this sky, these ascending hawks. I have heard Bach and Beethoven. I've listened to choirs in the cathedrals of Europe. What I heard that morning was more beautiful. It made me want to cry, shout, and beg forgiveness. It made me want to run back down the road.

9

WALKING IN THE WOODS

FOR A WHILE AFTER I met Jeffrey Funk, I refrained from calling him about my grandfather's gun. This was partially because I didn't know the man and worried about asking for so much help, but also because I thought that the Smith & Wesson's end should be preceded by ceremony. It seemed important to mark the transformation, but I could not think what form that honoring should take.

Lacking any model for such a ritual, I began asking questions of people around me, particularly the ones who had experience with cultures other than my own. That's how I ended up talking with Germaine White.

Germaine and I had met twelve years before when I managed the ranch on Dry Cottonwood Creek and she was working as the director of outreach and education for the Confederated Salish and Kootenai Tribes. The ranch, which was owned by a conservation group called the Clark Fork Coalition, was undergoing a Superfund cleanup to remediate damage done to the Clark Fork River's floodplain by copper mining. Because the river runs through the ancestral territory of the Salish and Kootenai, Germaine had come to represent her tribes on the Clark Fork Coalition's board of directors.

She was good at her job, having a calm, kind, thorough way of talking with people. A particular courtesy emanates from Germaine. In the intervening years, I've wondered precisely how to describe that power of hers. The nearest I can get is to say that it is rooted in a presumption of mutual respect. Where she goes, decorum follows. It's a visible phenomenon—a halo of good behavior engulfing people near her. To stand within the circle is to know with absolute certainty that Germaine will treat you with the decency due every human being and that you, if you are a worthwhile creature, must take the same approach with her. When she sits up straight, you will, too.

I sat up that way more than a decade ago when I attended a Clark Fork Coalition board meeting to report on the various projects of the Dry Cottonwood Creek Ranch. Germaine was at the far end of a conference table, one smallish salt-and-pepper-haired Native American woman in a room full of white entrepreneurs, conservationists, and fishing guides.

Winter was just beginning when I came to that meeting. I was working hard to finish the barndominium, my ad hoc home on the range. Between reporting on the cattle herd and a revegetation project, I described my progress toward putting a proper roof over my head. By springtime, I told everyone, the place would be ready. Several board members nodded approvingly. They checked the project's budget, shuffled papers, and prepared to move on.

"Where are you living while you work?" Germaine asked.

She had seen the tack room, I think. She knew it was a ply-wood box that only complete destruction could have removed the smell of pack rat urine from. When I replied that I was living there, a silence followed that seemed to embarrass everyone except Germaine.

I recall this much of the subsequent conversation: She did not like the fact that, with winter brewing, I was sleeping on a futon ringed with space heaters. It upset her to learn that I cooked in a toaster oven that tripped the breaker nightly and that I washed dishes at the yard hydrant. She understood that even a ranch manager needs to keep warm and fed.

Something about her concern stuck with me when the meeting was over. It stayed in my mind while I bought the week's groceries and supplies. On the homeward drive, as I sped out on Interstate 90 from tight ravine country onto the grassland near Drummond, I realized what it was: My mother would have asked the same question in the same way.

After I left Dry Cottonwood and Germaine finished her term on that board, we have crossed paths many times. I came to her for advice when I began to work on grizzly conservation projects with the Confederated Salish and Kootenai Tribes. I borrow her rototiller when it's time to turn our garden, and she never lets me leave without a jar of black currant or huckleberry jam. All of the time we've known each other, she has been generous with me.

Her house sits at the base of the Mission Range at the elevation where mountains become valley. Like Gillian and me, she lives very near the dividing line between cultivated land and ancient forest. We live on different sides of that line, though: Germaine's house is tucked into the trees. Ours stands a little way into the farmland.

On an unexpectedly warm spring day, I drove north from our farm to Germaine's for two reasons: because she was having trouble with the electric fence that keeps bears out of her berry patch and had asked me to fix it, and because I wanted to continue a discussion that we had begun some weeks before. I'd told her about the gun and my plan to change it into an object with different qualities. We'd spoken a little then about the role of firearms and violence in the history of this place. Germaine had told me about the 1908 Swan Valley Massacre that occurred when a Montana game warden attacked a party of eight tribal members hunting near the reservation. The hunters were exercising rights guaranteed to them by the 1855 Treaty of Hellgate. They carried a signed statement of permission from the Flathead reservation's Indian agent as well as licenses issued by the state. They had, in other words, cleared the expedition with the authorities in every way possible.

The warden, Charles Peyton, still wanted them gone. He rode into camp and harassed the hunters, then returned the following morning with a deputy. In an ensuing confrontation, Peyton killed three men and a thirteen-year-old child, and was wounded by one of the hunters. The deputy fled. A woman in the hunting party, Clarice Paul, saw the warden reloading his gun and pulled her husband's rifle from beneath his dead body. She shot Peyton and killed him.

This is recent history. Clarice Paul was pregnant at the massacre. Her son, John Peter Paul, lived long enough for Germaine to know him well.

It was the first I had heard of the massacre, though I had been many times to the Swan Valley and even hunted there. That story filled me with pain, anger, and a sense of racial guilt. The warden, of course, was white. The surname Peyton, like Andrews, comes from the British Isles. A sense of distant common roots filled me with a feeling of inherited complicity. It hung at the back of my mind as I headed north to Germaine's.

A few miles beyond the town of St. Ignatius, I drove uphill through the Mission Dam tribal homesites. There were many joyful children jumping on trampolines, playing on porches, riding double down the road on ATVs.

Germaine's is the uppermost house in the neighborhood. Straight east, the land steepens toward 9,400-foot-tall West Saint Mary's Peak. Mission Creek and its flanking trees point westward across the valley floor. Big carnivores use the riparian cover to move across the valley. The same is true of the smallest birds.

Her back deck overlooks the valley. That afternoon, I walked around the side of the house to find Germaine at her outdoor table in animated conversation with a young dark-haired woman. Greeting me, Germaine introduced Ruth Miller as her niece, a climate and indigenous rights activist, and a member of the Dena'ina Athabaskan tribe. Ruth had an open, direct manner; made unflinching eye contact; and seemed altogether at home in her skin. It seemed possible to me that she might change the world.

At Germaine's urging, I began explaining what I was trying to do. I described the revolver to Ruth and told her how it had come to me from my grandfather.

Germaine nodded. "I have objects like that," she said. "Things that come with a set of responsibilities."

I told them that I had settled on the idea of unmaking the gun and turning it into something else. Ruth asked me to explain why. It was an open question demanding the most complete answer I could muster.

"It has to do with my family," I said. "My ancestors." I found it hard to continue. I had seldom used the words *my ancestors* in conversation.

We were sitting on three sides of the table, Germaine across from me, Ruth at the end. I looked from one to the other. Both women were watching me closely. Working a crescent of dirt loose from under my thumbnail, I had the feeling that comes before diving into water: an unmistakable sense of jumping off, worries about hidden stones.

I gave the short version: that my father's people had come on the *Mayflower*; that generations of my family, like most colonists, had sucked the marrow from a rich and thriving continent; that nearly everywhere I went I saw the avarice and blindness of my forebears reflected in violence done to Native cultures and the natural world; that I had come to see how my antecedents had been taking things by force for centuries, striving blindly in their own interests, giving precious little back.

That history had everything to do with weapons and power, I told Germaine and Ruth, some measure of which had come down to me with my grandfather's revolver. There was the heart of it: The .357 felt like a weapon of conquest in my hands.

"That," I said, "is not what I want to give my children."

I told them how I proposed to turn my grandfather's weapon into a tool meant for different work, treating that action as a first step toward unmaking the violent inheritance that comes—in the form of a gun and otherwise—to settlers' sons. By hammering one thing into another, I would forge a beginning and equip myself for better labor to come.

"One thing keeps tripping me up," I said. "It's hard to destroy anything that was handed down—that came as a gift."

"You know," Germaine said, "it's only European culture that looks at fire as a destructive force. Fire belongs to hell in their cosmology. Fire consumes things. It uses them up. But Indigenous people, not just the Salish but a lot of bands and tribes around here, saw fire differently. We used fire to burn underbrush and keep the forests healthy. It was a tool—our biggest, most useful tool—of renewal. It was something given to us, to be used in taking care of the landscape.

"This idea of yours with the gun—it's not in Salish tradition. You're not part of the Salish tradition. But I can say this: Since this is about people who came before you, it's important to honor your ancestors in whatever you're going to do. Think about them. Be grateful. If this is about family, talk to yours. Ask them what they think of what you're doing."

That felt right. For weeks, I had been wondering what my mother and father would make of the idea taking shape in my mind. I had been thinking of them often, at times glimpsing them with unprecedented clarity across the distance that opens between grown children and parents. In such moments, I thought that I could discern their essential strengths: the discipline and personal fortitude implied by my father's turn away from war; the rare, unflinching acuity of my mother's eye.

"We have this idea, in Salish culture, of preparing the feast," Germaine said. "It's about the work that comes before an event, a ceremony, or anything important. The preparation is just as important as what happens at its end. You've been preparing this feast for years. You've lived here most of your adult life, and you've been paying attention. I know that about you. You pay attention and have a good heart. The ceremony can be your own. Whatever you decide to do will be right.

"You love this place," she said, looking straight at me, sounding sure. "This is your *home.*"

I had been fourteen years in Montana. I had ridden horses and hunted in the mountains. I had slept many nights under the enormous star-flecked sky. For all that, in the deepest recesses of my heart and mind, I had not dared to call the place home. To hear her say it gave me strength and purpose.

"Dena'ina people have a coming-of-age ceremony," Ruth said. "And in some ways, that's what this sounds like. A moment of maturity, consideration, and growth. The difference, maybe, is that it's a coming-of-age ceremony for a family line."

"Honor the thing," Germaine said, nodding. "Honor the object and the past, and all the people who lived and died to put you in this world. Honor them even if you don't agree with them—even if you're going to go a different way from them. Give them your best then let go of what you can."

It was past midafternoon, the weather so fair and warm that we left the table, walked out to the lawn, and sat on newly greened grass in a patch of sun.

"The last two hundred years have been full of misunderstanding and disconnection," Germaine said. "There has been an enormous cultural collision. Now is the time to build bridges between peoples, and between humankind and the rest of nature. You're wise to be thinking about this and to be asking these questions of Native people."

Soon, Ruth said goodbye and carried on down the road. Germaine walked me to the berry patch, where I tinkered with electrical connections, tested the fence's current with a voltmeter, and fixed a place where a hot wire was shorting out. The fence ran well when I was through.

"When it comes to ceremony," Germaine said, while I loaded tools into my truck, "some things are just inherently good. Sage is good. Sweetgrass is good. Red cedar is good."

I understood. For as long as I've been alive, without knowing why, I've felt better with those plants around. Every few years, my mother gives me braided sweetgrass for the cab of my truck. She likes the smell. Passing through cedar groves, I roll leaves between my fingers, bring my hands to my nose, and take the good, wild scent into my lungs. Before I came to live in Montana, I would collect sage on road trips, bind it with string, and bring it home to the rainy coast of Washington. I kept the bundles until they lost their smell and shattered. I told Germaine as much.

"I'm not surprised," she replied. "Like I said, you pay attention."

Going inside the house, she returned with jam and a handful of cedar sprigs.

"Whatever you decide to do," she told me, "take these."

ONE COLD DAY SHORTLY after that conversation, I buckled the revolver around my waist, packed a sleeping bag into my camping pack, and walked uphill from our house. Cutting through the Triangle, I kept a close eye on thicker patches of brush. A grouse flushed from underfoot, making a racket like a two-stroke engine starting up. I climbed on, always upward, farther into the forest with the gun a weight on my hip.

A quarter mile up a steep grown-in logging road, I found old tins and bottles half buried in the duff. One piece of trash—a well-preserved can with the single word CHICKEN and a bird's silhouette in black ink—caught my eye. Shaking it clean, I tucked the tin into my pack and went on.

From the road's end, ducking limbs and clambering over the trunks of fallen trees, I dropped back down to the course of Agency Creek. The channel was braided and its movements had scoured a clearing thirty paces wide. There were bars of raw gravel and overhanging cutbanks. The dead hulks of trees lay half submerged. Clouds scudded across a round blue patch of sky, the place still and silent except for the sound of water.

I chose a mossy spot beside the bank and took off the revolver. I had brought along the cartridge belt, too, its leather loops full of the old rounds that had come with the gun. The brass casings

had blued with the waxy corrosion of age. I set myself to cleaning them, a thing I had long meant to do but never had time for.
One at a time, I pressed the bullets free of their leather keepers.
With the back of a knife blade and a smooth river stone, I scraped
them clean. Corruption fell away in flakes, revealing bright metal.
I worked at the job for the better part of an hour until my fingers
took on a tinge and the ammunition formed a pile on the ground.
Though I did not know if the rounds would fire, I put them back
in place, washed my hands in snowmelt, and buckled the cartridge belt on.

Taking the littered can from my pack, I crossed the clearing and
set it on a fallen log, chicken side toward me. I turned and walked,
counting paces. At twenty, I turned around.

I stood there, deep in the woods, a gunslinger staring down a
tin that shone like a sheriff's badge. I unholstered the gun, loaded
all six chambers, thumbed the hammer back, and took aim.

When I fired from twenty yards away, the can shuddered and an
echo rang through the forest. Two ravens startled from the treetops
and crossed the patch of open sky, calling roughly as they climbed.

Walking over, I found a hole dead center through the chicken's
black breast. It was a bull's-eye, a lucky, perfect, killing shot that
far better marksmen than I am would struggle to re-create. My
hand had been steady. The revolver, after so many years, shot true.

I went on firing, hitting the tin in every way I could think of:
from the hip, one-handed, in a hurry. I shot many times in quick
succession, and the can jumped like a rabbit along the ground. I
shot until the barrel warmed and the shells were almost spent.
After three decades of waiting, every cartridge fired.

For the first time in a long while, I found joy in the revolver.
It was a very, very fine weapon—perfectly balanced and without
the unpleasant kick of most handguns. It fit my hand as if made

for me. I let myself enjoy the tool's power and precision, exalt and glory in noise and smoke, and be proud of how I could make the can leap from its log and fly. Alone in the mountains, I made a commotion. I celebrated my grandfather's gun. Wild things listened for miles around.

With the last six rounds, I slowed down and took careful aim. My hand was tired. I hit the can three times out of five then stopped. A single live cartridge remained in the gun.

Raising my hand, I pointed the Smith & Wesson toward a bare-soil bank at the base of a thickly timbered slope. I aimed the gun generally but did not focus on the sights. Instead, I studied the thing in my hand. I tightened my finger on the trigger and watched the hammer begin to rise. The cylinder advanced, moving with a neat click. The hammer climbed higher, to the point of springing free. When it did, the pin snapped forward, almost too fast for my eye to follow. Smoke exploded from the barrel and breech. A shadow leapt from the muzzle.

The report echoed along Agency Creek. When it passed away, the sound of moving water competed with a ringing in my ears. I felt light-headed and realized that I had been holding my breath after I set my finger on the trigger. Gulping clean, cold air, I studied the gun. Its bullets were spent. A wisp of smoke remained. When it was gone, the thing in my hand was only steel.

I climbed up and up to a ridge that runs back toward McCleod Peak, the highest point in the Rattlesnake National Recreation Area and Wilderness. Following the spine as far as I could, picking my way through snowdrifts that hadn't yet noticed spring, I came to where the Jocko primitive area begins. Short of that line, I found a mostly level spot where I could look up toward the heights and down to the valley below. Through breaks in the timber, I could see our farm and some neighboring homesteads.

I set stones in a fire ring and gathered wood. It was nearly dusk, and when a night breeze came out of the southwest, I pulled on all the clothing I had brought. It was early in the year for sleeping out. I had climbed higher than was prudent for the season.

It had rained, so I had to hunt under snags and stones for tinder. I worked through several sizes of branches until I achieved a durable blaze. I was hungry, but having resolved not to eat, contented myself with tending the fire. I fortified my hearth against the wind with rough-stacked stones.

Removing the gun from its holster, I set it between my crossed legs and the flames. A handful of dry needles tossed on the coals created a brief bright flaring in which I could see every detail. I examined the revolver this way, five seconds at a time, in the flickering glare of a pine-needle fire.

Strip away the violence and harm this gun can do, I thought, *and what's left is uncommonly pretty.* The precision, care, and utilitarian beauty evident in well-made firearms are rare in the world. Unlike most things, such weapons are meant to last. They are built to pass through generations.

By the inconstant fire, I could barely see the seam that separated one half of the revolver's frame from the other. It was a perfect joint, so subtle that my thumbnail skated over it without catching at all. I had owned the gun for nearly ten years but had never taken the thing apart.

In the flaring glow, I considered how often and completely I had trusted the obscure tiny interior parts to do their jobs. If a bear had charged me, I'd have lifted my hand and presumed that each cog and flange would move just so, nudging its neighbor into action. It seemed oddly credulous that people trusted such a contraption in emergencies.

Running a fingertip across the gun's curving, cold perfection, I found it hard to picture the facility where such a thing could be made. I'd carried with me a rough-forged piece of metal, a dull-gray, fire-scaled, four-inch-long scrap I had been practicing on. It was like a small dog's tongue. I hadn't meant to bring the scrap into the mountains, but it had stowed away in a pocket of my work pants. Holding this beside the Smith & Wesson, I found it difficult to believe that the two objects shared a parent material.

But there was an elemental relation. Any wrought-metal thing, no matter how fine or complicated, has its roots in a forge. The sleek modern world comes back, at bottom, to the hammer and hand.

It was full dark and cold enough that I drew so near the fire as to be looking almost straight down into it. Propping up my backpack for a windbreak on one side, I set two small parcels in its lee—Germaine's red cedar and a sweetgrass braid that my mother had left on my dashboard years ago.

I burned the plants little by little, letting each one catch, gutter, and smolder out in turn. I held the braid upwind so its coal end glowed like a cigar and aromatic smoke blew over the revolver and around me. For a long while, that's all I did—lit the end of a cedar branch or the braid, let it go out, smelled the good scent, and watched the smoke trail off in spirals. The sweetgrass was densely woven and burned slowly. The coals crept red and beautiful along the stems. They hardly changed the braid's shape but turned each blade of grass into a strand of bone-colored ash.

Smoke ribboned the darkness, flowing over my hands and the revolver. The smell—sweetgrass, cedar, sweetgrass—lingered around me.

I had no sense of time. It was night, that was all. Looking up from the fire, I found that I could not see stars or the trees around me. This gave me the sense of being utterly, terrifyingly alone in the mountains in the way that drives people to look over their shoulders and clutch their weapons tightly.

The gun, loaded, would have been a comfort, but I found that I could think clearly without it in the silence. I could remember the words "This is your *home*."

A person should not fear their home. Such fear, I think, is related to our deepest troubles. Setting the gun down, with the smoking hank of sweetgrass in hand, I stood and walked off from the fire. My boots were visible for a few steps, then vanished into perfect blackness. I went on, stumbling, heart racketing against my ribs with an unexpected panic. I felt terribly vulnerable, conscious of the insane fragility of life: the thin-walled veins and splitting cells; the faint, precise electrical impulses that make a mind; the unconscious symphonies that kept up while I slept. I knew how quickly teeth or claws could end that music. I could hear my heart clearly in the forest. Each beat was proof that it could stop.

Fear gripped me so hard that I almost could not breathe, just as it had when I first worked on the Sun Ranch and found myself alone in the mountains. It was on me like a pouncing cat—an old panic, a strain of night terror passed down through generations of white settlers in the Americas. It was a colonial fear, born of the creeping suspicion that the continent did not want my kind and might well swallow me up. *What kind of fool*, it screamed, *stands in the wilderness unarmed?*

I wanted to stoke a head-high blaze. I wished for a house to enter, a door to bar, a wall to sit against so nothing could creep up behind me. More than anything, I wanted to load the gun and hold it until daybreak.

How many times had I carried that weapon as a talisman against fear? I saw the revolver in my mind's eye: laying on the passenger seat of a ranch truck while I chased down a midnight poacher, hanging heavy at my waist as I pushed through underbrush and bear smell toward a steer's carcass from which the ear tag had to be retrieved, cold in my hand the night our neighbor called to say a man was walking up the gravel road shooting.

When a person stands alone at night in the mountains, everything draws near. Doubts circle. Terror is a sound or step away. But strength, a kind of subtle and durable fortitude, is just as close at hand.

I called my parents often in the days leading up to my excursion, asking each of them separately for their opinion on what I was doing. I wanted their advice.

My mother said it was important for me to spend time with the gun, to be alone with it before I undertook its transformation. She wanted me to look closely, take the time necessary to study it with my whole mind. That council, in large measure, is what steered me toward the mountains.

She asked me to connect with the thing I meant to destroy. I had done so. Down along the creek, I had gloried in the gun's accuracy—its precision and power. In uneven firelight, I had enjoyed its seamless beauty and marveled at the fact that human hands could do such fine work.

My father was more direct in his response. He admired the path I was on, and said so plainly. The notion that I might, through hard work, change the revolver into something entirely different engaged him. It was, he said, both an act of nonviolence and an attempt at making art. In the last of our conversations, I asked him what my grandfather would think.

For a time, the phone was silent against my ear. "I don't know," he said finally. "I just don't know. He'd like the way you're working with your hands. He'd like how you treat the land around the farm.

That would all make sense to him. He'd respect the work you've put into this whether he agreed with what you were doing or not. Given what he must have seen in the war, I'd like to think that part of him would approve of there being one less gun in the world. But I don't know. He never talked about those things to me."

The braid in my hand still smoldered, releasing a thin white streamer. I lifted it higher so the smoke broke around my face. The scent warmed and comforted me. It was a burning piece of summer, and I held it as tightly as I had gripped the revolver on other nights.

I waited, shivering, to see if the mountains would stop my heart. After a while, I found that I could see some way into the forest. The trunks and stones were faint colorless shapes. An owl called from down below. Stars and the moon's rising crescent showed through the pines.

I stood motionless, sweetgrass in hand, its smoke licking out through the trees. I was colder than a person should let himself get when he is alone.

It took time—many breaths and several minutes—for my panic to subside. As the fear ebbed, though, I felt certain that something different remained in its place. I went to the fire, warmed my bones, and wondered what the new thing was.

Before I ever wanted to become a cowboy, I dreamed of being Indian. A common and impossible white boy's dream, I know. It had
something to do with my mother reading me a condensed children's version of Henry Wadsworth Longfellow's "The Song of
Hiawatha" so many times that, even now, if someone were to wake
me, saying: "By the shores of Gitchee Gumee, by the shining Big-
Sea-Water," I could answer without pausing: "Stood the wigwam
of Nokomis, daughter of the Moon, Nokomis." I loved Hiawatha.
The fact that Longfellow stood outside the culture he meant to
render is not lost on me.

It had something to do with my mother's father claiming a
distant connection to the tribes of the Blackfoot Confederacy.
He never proved the link, though his surname, Chartier, features in marriage records between French Canadian settlers
and members of several tribal groups. Grampi, as we called
him, searched various archives for some link to an indigenous
past, scouring church and courthouse records in the towns from
which his Quebecois ancestors moved south and westward.
He went to Chartierville and Trois-Rivières but found nothing
more promising than missing information—gaps that he filled
with conjecture. My grandmother remained unconvinced.

Each summer when I was a child, my parents would settle
me between sleeping bags and a cooler in the back seat of our

car and motor across the Cascades, past the basalt scablands of eastern Washington, through the claustrophobic forests of the Idaho panhandle, and finally into Montana. We made many versions of that trip, but the one I remember best took place when I was eight years old. That year, we drove to the Black Hills and the Little Bighorn.

It was an August afternoon and I remember hot wind across an expanse of grass and the white markers scattered in the hills. The place was still known then as the Custer National Battle-field, and most of the visitors went straight to the rise where the colonel and his men died. They wanted to see where the doomed hero had fallen, take a picture with his stone. We went there, too; but afterward, we walked near the river where Lakota, Northern Cheyenne, and Arapaho people had been camped.

The battlefield howled with loss—not only of men, women, and children in the heat of war, but also of the destruction of a way of living. Even a child could see that the land thereabouts was as challenging as it was beautiful. The wind gave no quarter. The sun was high and relentless. The knee-high grass looked to be parching by the hour.

The fact that people had survived there through summer and bitterest winter, blizzard and drought, impressed me deeply. Thriving between grass and sky for thousands of years, they had made lives without ruining the place that sustained them. I respected that. It seemed to me that the tribes had been on the right side of things and the US Army in the wrong. Perhaps my parents presented matters this way. Maybe I decided for myself.

I made a coup stick on that trip. Having read about the plains tribes' practice of earning honor by counting coup on enemies, I peeled a willow branch and used my father's fly-tying supplies to adorn it with bands of tightly wrapped colored thread and a clump of pheasant tail feathers. I worked hard on the project and kept the stick on my lap as we drove across the prairie. I carried it through the thickets surrounding each place where we camped. Knowing that such an implement could only be used on suitable foes, I nurtured hopes of coming across a lone and unsuspecting bison or perhaps a bear. I took the stick seriously. It was as sacred as anything I owned at the time.

It makes a picture: a small, round, pale-faced Seattle boy anointed with sunscreen skulking through the brush of a AAA campground, hoping he might prove to be the unlikely but true heir to a knowledge and a way of living that seemed—I knew no living Indian people then—to have vanished from the land. I passed a week like that.

When we arrived on the Zentz Ranch, though, I hid the stick away. It seemed impractical, even silly, to count coup on cattle and tractors. I was ashamed to carry the stick in the company of Pat, Suzie, and their three capable boys. The change was so sudden and complete that I mistook it for growing up. After that, I wanted to become a cowboy.

The two dreams—cowboy, Indian—had elements in common: animals and sky, a sense of general self-sufficiency, entanglement with a landscape that had claimed my heart. Enough resemblance existed between them that I had no trouble mapping one onto the other. That is what I did. I began to pretend that one lifeway was an extension of the other and that the same kernel of wisdom lay at the heart of both.

It was an easy shift and a common one with ample precedent. Over the last two centuries, white settlers of the American West have excelled at such overwriting. We have convinced ourselves, wrongheadedly, that our agriculture is a suitable, logical, and sufficient replacement for what it has obliterated or displaced. It is a grave error.

For my own part, I'm embarrassed at how long it has taken me to notice that a rancher's view of the natural world is blindered in comparison to a hunter's perspective; that driving livestock from one field to another is nothing like stalking free-ranging herds; that the work of finding, gathering, and preparing a hundred different wild plants bears no resemblance to growing alfalfa or oats; that most tribal lives unfold in atmospheres of intense community and with a collective belief in the long future while too many modern agriculturalists sit alone in tractor cabs, convinced that the best times are gone; that it matters whether a culture chooses profit or perpetuity for its goal.

My friend Germaine talked once about the importance of noticing and cultivating the reciprocal relationship between humans and the rest of the natural world.

She said: "Reciprocity is not the same as sustainability. White people talk about sustainability, which has to do with how much you can take from nature, or a place, without it falling completely apart. There are good things about that attitude—or, at least, it's an improvement over taking everything without thinking of the consequences, but there are ways in which it misses the point."

We were sitting on her porch in summer. A magpie settled in the fruit trees, checked the unripe plums, and flew on.

"I look, and most Native people look, at the relationship between people and their place in terms of reciprocity. The question then becomes: What can I give back? What can I do to take care of the place that feeds and shelters me? That's a very different approach than asking: How much can I sustainably take?"

Salish, Kootenai, and Pend d'Oreille people have been asking what they could give these lands for millennia. In recent years, they have found one answer in the work of ecological restoration. Anytime I look north across the Jocko Valley, I see the fruit of their labors. The river, once straightened, denuded, and channeled in places, now meanders unbroken through willow stands and cottonwoods. Wild animals follow its course. A recovering population of bull trout spawns in the highest tributaries.

I cannot join a tribe. I can, however, walk along the Jocko— through stands of broomstick-thick willows, new cottonwoods, and burgeoning chokecherry groves that the Confederated Salish and Kootenai Tribes have preserved or painstakingly restored—and recognize good work. I can be grateful for what the tribes have done in this valley, take up similar labor, and advance it as far as I am able.

On our farm, water rises to the surface just downhill from where the forest gives way to grass. It is an intermittent workaday stream, dry in winter. Even in the runoff season, when the flow quickens, the spring remains narrow enough to step across. Cattle have caved in the banks. For the quarter mile between where the spring rises and where it sinks into the ground near our north fence, nothing grows but grass. For decades, livestock have not suffered saplings.

In the first months of 2020, I visited the spring often. One afternoon, I realized that before someone cleared the little watercourse to suit the tastes of livestock it would have been flanked by brush and trees. It would have been like the triangle of thick tangled vegetation beyond our farm's uphill fence—a haven for wild creatures.

It had been that way, I decided, and could become so again. Like the Jocko River in the valley below, it could be restored. The only things lacking were work and proper tools.

I stood by the channel, finally sure of my course: I would make my grandfather's Smith & Wesson into a tree-planting spade, a tool meant for resurrecting forests. Armed with that implement, I could give something back to the place that was my home.

I could bring the farm's small battered watercourse back to life by planting seedlings, opening the soil for them until my arms ached in their sockets. Water and time would raise groves and thickets. There would be songbirds, bedded deer, and countless other creatures. For a while, that green future was so clear that it hung before my eyes. In it, I saw a chance to follow, in miniature, the example of the tribes.

10

THE NEW AGRARIAN SCHOOL

ON A CLEAR, COLD morning, I drove up the east shore of
Flathead Lake, glancing when I could from the two-lane highway
toward an expanse of water as blue as the sky. The lake was low.
When I came to Bigfork, I could see the pale shoreline stretching
northwest.

Jeffrey Funk's workshop, which he calls the New Agrarian
School, occupies the kind of graceless metal building that exists
everywhere on the landscape nowadays, which the unconscious
mind edits out of panoramas. Within, it is a wonderland.

The first thing I noticed were the power hammers. The place's
exterior door opened straight onto one of the larger examples:
a huge hunk of cast metal, half again taller than I was, with the
aspect of an open jaw.

"Five-hundred-pound Chambersburg," Jeffrey said, catching
me staring as we entered the shop. I said the thing looked heavier.
Five hundred pounds, he clarified, was not the machine's weight
but that of its striking element—the pneumatic ram that rose
and fell within the tool's curved arbor. The whole Chambersburg

forging hammer weighed more than five tons and required a two-foot-thick foundation to keep it from shattering the concrete floor. At rest and separated from each other by a few inches, the machine's anvil and upper die looked like a pair of huge molars. They got me to thinking about what a quarter ton of hardened steel could do to an errant hand.

There were many power hammers in Jeffrey's shop, small and large, each with a particular function. Some had rounded dies for spreading metal, and others, like the Chambersburg, had a flat hammer and anvil that came together like a jaw. Forges stood along the walls, each hooked to a gas line and exhaust stack. A network of air hoses, gas pipes, and ductwork overspread the space above us.

Once I was inside that high-ceilinged, white-walled building, it was impossible to look anywhere without stumbling across a trace of Jeffrey's craftsmanship and effort. To one side were racks of handmade hammers. Many anvils sat prettily and solidly on pedestals carved from tree trunks. Even the floor was beautiful, made of tongue-and-groove wooden blocks with their end grain showing and darkly patinaed by use. Having just the faintest hint of spring and give, it was the sort of floor that a person could work all day on.

The shop's true wonder was that—excepting the anvils and hugest pieces of equipment, things so heavy that they had to be cast or forged in factories—Jeffrey had made damn near everything himself. He had shaped the hundreds of hammers, punches, and tongs. He had built the racks where the tools hung. He had designed and constructed the propane forges ranked along the walls and all but the largest power hammers.

Everything in the building, from the largest anvil to the small-est punch, was beautifully made and impeccably maintained. The hammers' faces were burnished by use. In their precision, quality, and practicality, the tools reminded me of my grandfather's gun.

What Jeffrey did with those tools—the ways in which he made the world's harder materials bend gracefully to his will—was astounding. In one back corner was a pitchfork in progress, its tines sweeping in several directions like a bouquet of snakes. Jeffrey had left the project unfinished, a demonstration of how a single billet of metal could become a long-fingered implement. Like much that I saw at the New Agrarian School, the fork was a simple implement meant for a simple task, elevated by a devilishly complex process of creation.

In a smaller secondary room, a handmade cart held finished hand tools meant for sale. There were black-patinaed hatchets and hoes, axes and three-tined weeders, plus smith's hammers in several sizes and shapes. Jeffrey showed me the tools in passing, moving along to a countertop covered with stones. The rocks were not precious, but he had worked magic on them.

The first rock that drew my attention was softball-size and dark. ANDESITE read a piece of masking tape on the side, 2250 DEGREES. A small decorative steel tripod had been pressed halfway through the stone. Where each metal leg entered, the rock had bowed inward. I could see that the basalt had not been drilled or chipped away. It had moved like taffy or butter under a thumb to accommodate the metal, and still retained the look of malleability. It was an impossible thing—the sword in the stone.

Glancing at the white-haired, bright-eyed man beside me, I found him grinning.

"Temperature and pressure," Jeffrey said. "Same way it happens underground."

He had a fine, clear way of describing tools and processes. When he spoke about tempering metal, for example, he said that steel was an alloy of elemental iron with minute but important leavenings of carbon and other metals and that those elements were not simply contained in the iron but formed unique compounds in response to time, temperature, and mechanical forging.

"You can think of the steel's chemistry as being analogous to DNA," he said. "And the heat treatment as the 'nurture' that affects that chemistry's expression."

He further explained that hardness and toughness were the two essential qualities of good steel. Hardness let a piece of metal hold its edge while toughness gave it the ability to flex or take an impact without breaking. A blacksmith, Jeffrey told me, used heat and hammers to balance these opposing properties in a tool.

When I handed him the Smith & Wesson, he did not hold it by the grips as I had expected but took the barrel in one hand and the cylinder in the other. He turned the weapon this way and that, like a grocery shopper scrutinizing an apple. It was metal, raw material. He hefted the thing, tapped it with a ruler from the pocket of his tattered canvas pants. He ran a finger along the underside of the barrel, slipped the cylinder's catch, and swung it out.

"It must be good steel," he said. "Probably 4140 or something with more chromium."

Walking off with the revolver still gripped by the barrel and hanging at his side, he set the gun on an old-fashioned balance and slid scale weights—pounds, then ounces—from one side to the other.

"What do you think?" I asked him after a while. "Is it possible?"

A sour look crossed his face—the only time I'd seen one there. "Possible? Of course. It's just going to take a lot of work."

For a moment, neither of us spoke. I was looking for a graceful way to offer Jeffrey money for his time, experience, and help. Having seen his shop, I was resolved to do my work there, under his direction from start to finish. Though we had not discussed the matter, I assumed that I would have to pay. Even so, I doubted if he'd go for such an arrangement. Jeffrey seemed busy. His world was full of works in progress. He was gearing up to teach a summer's worth of classes to students.

"I'll help you with this," he said, tapping the gun with a finger.

I started to speak. He lifted one hand, palm out. The knuckles were large, the lines of his palm black with the grit of his livelihood.

"I don't want money. Consider it a gift from the universe.

"Now," he continued, looking pleased again. "Tea."

While Jeffrey put the kettle on, his wife, Betsy, emerged from a greenhouse attached to the house's southern side. They made a pair: Where Jeffrey was something like a bow—bent by his work into a potent, ready arc—Betsy Funk reminded me of an arrow fixed upright in the earth. She was slim, with once-blond hair and a habit of standing very straight. She had an undeniable warmth and an easy way of talking, which perhaps came from years spent teaching health and physical education classes to high school and community college students. I felt about Betsy as I had about Jeffrey, which is to say that I liked and trusted her immediately without reservations.

They were good, complex, openhearted people—the kind of couple that anyone not overly sensitive to the sound of air hammers and angle grinding would want as next-door neighbors. In the space of fifteen minutes, we consumed a plate of homemade cookies, discussed several books, and lamented the state of the nation. Toward the end of that time, Betsy told me that she had recently returned from traveling around the world. The trip, she said, had been in memory of an adult daughter lost to brain cancer.

With what must have been an act of will, Betsy began describing places she had seen, people who had treated her well. She talked about Italy, France, and the fjords of Norway; good food and dancing in the streets; how her daughter had bequeathed the trip, requiring it of her. It struck me as a wise thing to leave a quest like that to a beloved person—to hand on a mission that would nudge a survivor toward the living world.

We talked about the gun. How it had come as an inheritance and how I had used it. They knew plenty about agriculture. Jeffrey, though a strict vegetarian, had worked ranches as a younger man. Betsy still kept her hand in growing things, planting enormous quantities of flowers that she sold at a farmers' market.

I told them about the farm that Gillian and I were starting, about our plans to grow raspberries, raise grass-fed beef, and sell it all locally. For a person who eschewed meat, Jeffrey was supportive. Perhaps this should not have surprised me, coming as it did from the founder of the New Agrarian School.

Ask Jeffrey Funk why he teaches workshops with names like Hand Tools for Farm and Garden, Making Axes, and Wild Iron—a class in which students drive to eastern Montana, dig hematite ore, cart it back in buckets, smelt it in a bike-powered furnace run on homemade charcoal, and forge the resulting metal—and he'll say he does it because it's interesting and the skills involved are becoming too rare. He will say that the craft of blacksmithing lies close to the heart of civilization but that small workshops have been replaced by industrial casting and forging. He will tell a story of twentieth-century scaling, modernization, and loss of artisanal knowledge that perfectly describes agriculture as I've mostly known it.

"You don't know how lucky you are," Betsy said, as I followed Jeffrey out the kitchen door toward the shop, "to have him help you this way."

She said the words levelly, stating a fact.

I stayed all day. Jeffrey and I talked over our plan for the gun. We looked closely at several of the hoes and spades in the shop. We discussed the gun, the mechanics of planting trees, and many other things. I never lifted a hammer. No furnace roared to life. Jeffrey sent me down the road with a reference book on archaic tools, a sheaf of large scratch paper, and instructions to begin sketching the tool I wanted to create.

"Anyone who wants to make things," he said, "should learn to draw."

One week later, I drove up the lake again in the early morning and unrolled the diagram I had made on a steel-topped table. It was a rough picture. I felt like a kid in art class.

As I had rendered it, the planting spade looked somewhat like a widened pickaxe. As Jeffrey pored over the sketch, I explained the qualities that I wanted the tool to have. It needed two cutting faces: one of them a hoe for clearing sod, the other a long narrow shovel for digging the holes necessary to plant saplings. I also wanted the tool to retain some visual element of its origin. When I picked the new creation up, I told him, I wanted to know that I was holding my grandfather's gift in my hand.

For just a moment, I worried that Jeffrey might consider this last demand unnecessary and sentimental. The approving, thoughtful look that crossed his face put me entirely at ease.

"This is drawn to scale?" he asked after some time. I said that it was.

"I think you'll want it bigger. We won't know until we make one, though."

Walking to one of the forges, he struck a flame, opened the gas line, and started the blower. The forge roared evenly, starting the long process of coming up to temperature.

Jeffrey pulled out his ruler and began measuring the sketch, recording the total length and width, checking the thickness of the eye.

"First, we need to know how much metal this tool requires."

He grabbed a finished garden hoe and laid it on his scale. After running the weights, he straightened up and turned to me.

"It'll be heavier than this, so we'll start with four pounds of steel. See where that gets us."

Jeffrey walked outside to the racks that held forging stock and selected a solid rod about three inches in diameter and several feet long. Lifting it with a grunt, he brought it to his band saw, measured a length calculated to yield a chunk of appropriate weight, and set the blade in motion. The saw cut slowly with a high and steady noise. We watched the teeth chew down through metal.

"This stock came out of an aluminum plant that closed down near Libby," he said. "It's incredible steel—tool-grade 4140 out of a machine they used to break the crust on pots of molten aluminum. I've got thousands of pounds. Enough to keep busy."

When the cut was made and a short cylinder rolled free, Jeffrey picked it up, walked to the forge, and opened the door. Using tongs, he pushed the steel into the howling yellow maw.

"Tea," he said, shutting the door. "That round stock takes a while to heat up."

While we drank, he explained in detail how the tool would be made. In blacksmithing, much depends on the order of operations. For example: If a smith wants to flatten the end of a piece of square stock and curl it into a pretty scroll, the flattening must precede the curling. With a more complex process like the forging of a tool, sequencing becomes crucial.

On scrap paper, Jeffrey began a list of steps. I kept and studied that list.

BEGIN 3 1/4" OF 2 3/8" Ø (ROUND STOCK) 4140—4
    LB. 2 OZ.
FORGE TO 1" X 2 1/2" X 5 5/8"
PUNCH THROUGH—1 1/4" PUNCH
FORGE EYE AREA TO MAKE SLOT 2 7/8"
BUTCHER 1/2 WAY THROUGH BOTH ENDS @ ≈ 1/2"
    FROM SLOT—NOTE TRANSITIONS
STEP DOWN W 1 1/4" BLOCK
FULLER BOTH ENDS TO ISOLATE MASSES

Without further explanation, he began working. Fetching a handful of tools from the wall, Jeffrey chose a set of tongs, pulled the yellow-hot cylinder from the forge, walked briskly to the five-hundred-pound Chambersburg, set his foot on a treadle, and gave the machine life.

The Chambersburg made two powerful sounds as it worked—a low, oily hiss as compressed air sent the hammerhead traveling upward in its guides and a round, dead, bass-drum thud when it struck a blow. It hit with earthshaking force, an impact that shut my eyes involuntarily until I grew used to it. The machine could move fast, striking twice in a single second, but Jeffrey used it judiciously. With careful movements of his foot, he could control how far and hard each hammer stroke would fall. More often than not, he'd land a single blow or a pair of them, then examine the results before going on.

He flattened two sides of the cylinder, transforming it into a bulge-ended rectangle. Throughout the process, he kept hold of the workpiece with long-handled tongs, adjusting its position minutely as the hammer fell. After thirty seconds, the metal faded from bright yellow to orange. Seeing this, he set the work on an anvil, measured its dimensions with his ruler, and tonged it back into the forge. Jeffrey repeated this process, sometimes pausing to square the ends and edges of the rectangle—he called it a blank—that he was making.

"Not bad," he said, after the metal's third session under the hammer. "One more heat and we're there."

For the next three hours, Jeffrey worked and I watched, realizing finally that he meant to show me the entire process start to finish. At two points in the work—punching and butchering—I held tools while Jeffrey struck them. Otherwise, I watched and did my best to understand the nuances of what he was doing. I took notes about how careful he was to make straight-sided rectangles and how he rested his heel against the ground when working a power hammer's treadle with his foot. I noticed the smooth steady way he slid a heated blank across the anvil, and I resolved to do likewise when my turn came.

What I could not grasp, though, was how he made progress so quickly. White-hot metal emerged from the forge, Jeffrey moved it subtly and briefly beneath the thudding power hammers and the material was changed. It stretched like taffy, humped like a breaking wave, spread into fish tails, and rose in ridges. By late afternoon, we sat in the shop drinking cold beer and watching a tool somewhat like the one in my mind's eye fade to black atop a heap of firebrick. That first tree spade, which was all Jeffrey's doing, was a beautiful, lightweight, snub-nosed thing. It had a six-inch-long shovel at one end, a four-inch-long hoe at the other, and was the spitting image of what I'd sketched on paper. The tool's eye had been spread into a pointed oval. Once the steel was cool enough to touch, I could not put it down.

"Take it home," Jeffrey said. "Carve a handle and use it for a while. It's not hardened, but that doesn't matter. You can come back and tell me what needs to change. You'll want it bigger and heavier. I know that much."

As I gathered my things, he handed me a softball-size lump of oil clay.

"Take this, too," he said. "And practice. It's soft, so you don't need a power hammer to move it around. Just put this on your anvil and knock it into shape. Make a blank, punch it through, and shape the spade and the hoe the same way I did. When you're done, make it back into a lump and start again."

I did as he suggested. Home on the farm, I carved a handle from hickory and used the tool to dig up and transplant lilacs. After a day at that work, I understood that the shovel was too short, the hoe too narrow, and the whole thing about two-thirds the size it needed to be. Working the oil clay faithfully and with mixed results, I found that I could square the stuff up well enough but that spreading it evenly was a challenge.

I undertook one other labor—combining Jeffrey's list of tasks and specs with my own notes and sketches so I had a comprehensive record of the first tool's creation. I was careful. I drew a detailed sketch to scale and made certain adjustments to the dimensions. I brought those sheets with me two weeks later when I drove back up to the New Agrarian School.

That morning, I arrived to find Betsy coming out of the house with a hamper full of cleaning supplies.

"I haven't cleaned like this since before the trip. Not since Kelsey died," she said. She was smiling. Her grandson, four years old and fiercely blond, followed at some distance.

In front of the shop, Jeffrey was grinding away one corner of what looked like a six-inch-thick headstone made of steel, showering the gravel with sparks. The metal rested horizontally before him at waist height across two of the sturdiest sawhorses I had ever seen.

Watching him, it struck me again that Jeffrey had been molded by his work. His hands were knobby and huge-knuckled. His mane of white hair, freed from the round bill-less cloth cap he often wore at work, began high on his forehead as if fire had singed it back. Over the course of his life, something had pressed his nose to the right in a clean, even sweep. It was a seamless bend, like iron struck by a smooth hammer. When he looked straight at me, the nose didn't quite align. It gave his fine-boned face a kind of gravitas.

There remained something indomitably youthful about his eyes, which were blue and brightened by insistent curiosity. When he took a glowing half-shaped tool from the fire and regarded it, his gaze held an unadulterated innocent interest. When he sat on an anvil to hold court or watch a disciple work, he swung his legs as if he were a child in a tree.

I hadn't seen a sixty-four-year-old do that. The fact that such joyous movement remained in Jeffrey told me something about how a person ought to live. Perhaps there was no mystery in it: It pleased him to make fine things and he made fine things all the time.

"You came here wanting to do a fairly difficult and technical piece of blacksmithing with basically no prior experience," he said to me, as we stood beside a seething forge.

He warned me that there was only one way to succeed at that in the time we had. Unlike the students who came to the New Agrarian School for two-week workshops, I would receive no formal lessons on craft or technique. I would not learn to run the forges well or spend time perfecting my hammering technique.

We would walk a narrower path where I would quickly learn to do a few things passably. Specifically, I would train with the medium-size power hammers. I would learn half the two-person task of drifting a tool's eye with punch and sledgehammer. I would practice shaping shovel and hoe blades by hand on the anvil. I would try to grasp, if not master, the art of forge welding.

This last skill—fusing two white-hot pieces of metal together with a series of precise and forceful hammer blows—was the most difficult and crucial step. For all its deadly precision, a revolver is a honeycomb. A hole runs through the barrel. Six more ventilate the cylinder. There are larger voids between the structural parts of the revolver's frame and within the trigger guard's arbor.

A tree spade, conversely, is solid and must remain so through years of heavy use. For one thing to become the other, Jeffrey and I would need to beat every bit of empty space out of the revolver. We would need to turn a convoluted hollow piece of metal into a simple solid one.

"We'll get to that later," Jeffrey said. "Try the hammers."

At the end of the day, which ran long, I drove home in the dusk with aching forearms and a half-finished, somewhat misbegotten iteration of the tool. Returning to Jeffrey and Betsy's place the following weekend, I finished it, made more changes to the design, and began again. We repeated the process three times. Each practice spade looked better than the last, but none were good enough. With every run-through, I managed to do more of the work without Jeffrey stepping in to correct something that was going too far wrong. He was an excellent and exacting teacher. Incompetence was hard for him to bear.

There was a step in the process where I had to spread thick metal into a fan shape. It was a tricky thing—fine work that I did not master quickly. I had to hammer outward from a centerline, leaving a thickened keel to give the finished blade its strength. I never could get that part right. When Jeffrey demonstrated it, the steel moved swiftly and evenly outward. The keel took shape with beautiful symmetry; it looked like the V-shaped frog beneath a horse's hoof.

Jeffrey got no peace while I tried to shape the frog. It took every ounce of his restraint to keep from grabbing the tongs from my hands.

"Back," he'd say. "Back, back! BACK! Get that hammer right in there and—NO-not-ON-the frog-NOT-ON-IT! Work outward. And back. Back at an angle from there. Hit it. HIT! Don't pet the fucking metal!"

I came to dread that part somewhat. It was the last of the steps that I could truly and irrevocably mess up. A bad blow could leave a lasting mark on the finished spade or crumple the all-important edges of the tool's eye.

I did not succeed in making the frog until my third practice run. Even then, I felt like I had gotten lucky. Jeffrey held the finished spade in his tongs, sighting along its backline.

"Not bad," he said. "You're ready."

Before coming to Jeffrey's, I saw the extraction of metal from the ground as an act of shortsighted violence. I looked at mining as smash-and-grab theft. It struck me as particularly bad because metal, unlike timber or grass, could not renew itself. Metal never grew back.

I said something like that to Jeffrey once. He agreed about the violence of mining—particularly the open pits and tailings of industrial mining—but went on to say that iron was the blood of everything. It ran through our veins and stone fissures in the earth, appearing in massive quantities, endlessly reusable. The grinding continental plates recycled it, hemorrhaging black basalt, exposing raw scabs of hematite ore.

We were sitting in what he called the library—a small beautiful cabin made of firebrick reclaimed from a defunct foundry. Its porch was held up by wrought-iron girders from a decommissioned bridge. Three of us—Jeffrey; my mother, who had come for a visit; and I—sat talking at dusk after a long day forging. Everything around us—steel brackets, hooks, shelves, reclaimed lumber—looked beautiful in its second or third life.

Stars make iron, Jeffrey told us. The universe is so ordered by the laws of physics that each sun uses increasingly heavy molecular fuels as it is born, grows, and dies. A star begins by burning lighter elements, like hydrogen and helium, in a process of *nuclear fusion. From there, it gets into the heavier stuff, working toward molecules with more atomic heft. Iron and nickel are as far as most large stars can carry the process. After that comes a stellar death of cooling and exhaustion then the massive explosion of a supernova. For this reason, iron is scattered everywhere in the cosmos.*

On Earth, he pointed out, the star metal is constantly recycled. If bent or broken, it can be melted down and made new. Heated, it can be beaten from one shape into another. Dissolved into rust, it rises again as ore. It runs through us every moment of our lives, though our bodies cannot make it. Our hearts pump iron, bound in hemoglobin, until they stop. Our blood is in a constant state of oxidation. Sometimes, Jeffrey said, it seemed like the stuff simply wanted to exist, get used, and be reborn.

11

A REFINING FIRE

IT WAS DUSK WHEN we reached Bigfork. Gillian and I hauled our bags to one of the cabins used by students and instructors when the New Agrarian School is in session, then we went out to meet Jeffrey and Betsy at a firepit behind the shop. They had a blaze going and we sat drinking whisky that I had brought as a gift, talking through the day to come.

"Tonight we'll anneal it," Jeffrey said, after darkness had fallen. "Tomorrow we go to work."

By this he meant that we would heat the gun and cool it slowly overnight in a bed of sifted wood ash to render the steel as malleable as possible.

"We could use a forge," he said. "But a wood fire is a better start. More traditional."

He stoked the flames, feeding in scraps of lumber that I recognized as waste from the process of carving handles.

"Whenever you're ready," he said.

Approaching the fire with the Smith & Wesson in hand, I was conscious of the weapon's delicacy. I had unscrewed and opened the revolver's frame the night before, revealing the imbricated workings of hammer and trigger. Even after I had put the gun back together, I went on thinking of it as fragile.

The coals glowed brightly. Looking at them, I could not see Gillian or the others' faces. For a while, the visible world was reduced to my upturned hands, my grandfather's revolver, and fire.

I was not alone. I had my grandfather in mind—his love of wild places. I thought of my parents, who first brought me out here. I remembered Germaine's good counsel: "You've been preparing this feast for a long time. Whatever you decide to do will be right."

I stood, fingers loosely around the gun, the backs of my hands hot. Taking up tongs, I grasped the revolver near its middle. I stretched out an arm and set the weapon in the fire.

A plume of sparks went up as embers shifted and settled. Licking flame hid the metal, so I could see only one curve of the cylinder and a sharp corner of the frame. The revolver hissed as its bluing bubbled and flashed to smoke. For a single instant, I wanted desperately to snatch the thing back.

As the cylinder lost its shine and coals settled around it, I felt different than I had while holding my grandfather's revolver above a crevasse or the black water of Puget Sound. My mind was on the future, not the past. I had no sense of something dying, only faith in the metal's vast potential.

As that fire burned, a weight lifted from me. I felt sure that I had begun the thing well. Leaning in, Jeffrey prodded the coals with a stick, nestling them around the barrel. We left the revolver that way for an hour or more.

We finished the heating process indoors in a forge, taking the metal up near two thousand degrees, far into the range of incandescence but below the point where steel begins to spark and burn away. We got it so damned hot that the gun glowed fiercely at the end of my tongs. When it had soaked in heat to Jeffrey's satisfaction, he brought out a medium-size metal trunk with buckles. It looked heavy, like a treasure chest. Laying it on a table, he instructed me to bring the gun from the forge.

I did so, returning to find the chest open and half full of gray-brown ash.

"Set it inside," Jeffrey said. "Bury it." He mimed flicking and scooping sand with his fingers.

I set the glowing, burning metal in and heaped ash around it. In the shop's half light, the gun's metal shone like a sunset. I watched the steel's color fade from yellow to orange as I covered it over until every inch was hidden.

When Gillian and I had retired to the cabin, we lay in bed talking. I told her how, when I first set the weapon in the fire, I had wanted to snatch it back.

"You regret it, then?"

I didn't. After the first moment's panic passed, I felt calm and unusually clearheaded. The four of us sat around the fire, talking, waiting for the gun to heat, while my mind returned to a single thought: that I was a very lucky man. I had received gifts from my family—the revolver, of course, but also sharp eyes and a strong heart. I had come to Montana and found a good life. I had driven a highway in a blizzard and met the woman I loved.

While the fire burned, I hardly considered the revolver. I thought instead about Gillian carrying our farm along, shouldering our daily work while I hammered steel and pursued notions. I thought about Jeffrey opening his shop and mind to a stranger. With these and other kindnesses filling my heart, there was no room for a sense of loss.

When the revolver went into the ash box and its steel cooled beyond the point of repair, the trigger was no longer capable of lifting the hammer. All temper gone from the mainspring, the firing pin was unable to fall. A fist unclenched in my chest. I breathed better than before.

I. CUT THIN SECTIONS ON BAND SAW: EIGHT 1/8" THICK SLICES OF BARREL; FOUR 1/4" THICK SLICES OF CYLINDER BLOCK.

Early in the morning, I exhumed the gun. The revolver's shape was exactly as it had been before, but every bit of luster had departed, leaving the metal dull gray, dusty, and blistered. Rust showed at the joints between moving parts and I had a strong urge to treat the spots with oil. The gun remained faintly warm. I pulled the trigger and nothing moved.

In a vise, I deconstructed it as far as I was able, opening the side plate and removing all the fine bits and pieces within. Jeffrey and I took the barrel and cylinder to a band saw, measured and clamped them, and began to cut.

The annealing had gone well. Swinging into motion, the blade cut smoothly if slowly. The cross sections made pretty shapes. Out near the mouth, they were wide-hipped, solid-bottomed figure eights. Farther in, where the cylinder's ejector rod nestled home, the shape became a numeral nine with a curling tail.

We cut the barrel, then the cylinder. Afterward, I spread the slices and other parts across the work-worn surface of an anvil. There were many inscrutable pieces. Even if the barrel had been whole, I could not have reassembled the gun.

---

2. CONSOLIDATE REVOLVER FRAME INTO A BILLET AND FORGE-WELD IT TO A BLANK OF 4140 TOOL STEEL.

Coming out of the forge, the frame was all curves and loops—a cursive letter I couldn't read. I struck the first blow—a light, precise hit meant to fold the frame in on itself, collapsing its members like a house of cards.

With each successive strike, I hit harder. The trigger guard bent. The sight lost its shape. The cylinder's housing began distorting forward and down. I held the tongs in one hand and struck with all my force, swinging from the shoulder, working the hammer up and down a piece of glowing steel that grew less recognizable with every strike. Jeffrey sat perched on the next anvil.

"Looking good," he said.

The hard work filled me with a fierce and rising joy. I beat the gun's frame on one side then the other, panting with effort, returning to the forge until I had reduced the thing to a thin uneven rectangle.

Rummaging near the back of the shop, Jeffrey fetched a coffee can with BORAX inked across the lid.

"Put this on" he told me, handing over a leather smith's apron. "Borax makes a mess and burns the shit out of skin, but you can't get a solid weld without the stuff."

He sprinkled a measure of granular white powder across the mass of folded compressed steel that I had created. Touching hot metal, the borax liquified and seeped into every crack. That was what made it useful. It filled the voids that we meant to close and join, keeping fire scale—oxidized iron that builds up on the outside of metal at high temperature—and other impurities from lodging there. If two pieces of very hot borax-drenched steel are hammered together with enough force, they become one.

I shut the forge door and waited, watching the thermometer climb through 2,150 degrees. The crumpled frame looked spectral when we pulled it out. At that heat, the light thrown off by the gun was a pure unalloyed white, like a star's.

Jeffrey insisted on doing the next step himself. The first unifying blows, the ones that would start the process of consolidating many layers of metal into a single forgeable blank, had to be struck perfectly.

He ran to the Chambersburg. Foot on the treadle, he sent the hammerhead up and brought it down with all its force on what had once been the revolver's frame. The ground shuddered. Molten borax flew in all directions, each bit of it tracing a glowing arc through the air. A drop landed between my cuff and glove, burrowing into my skin until I knocked it away.

When the metal had cooled somewhat, we examined it. The thing on the anvil was no longer a gun. It had become a piece of flat stock measuring about an inch wide and eight inches long. Faint seams could be seen on the surface, weaving this way and that, marking places where different layers and elements had been beaten together. Looking at them, I found that I could no longer tell what had been a trigger, an arbor, a housing, or a sight.

Because there was not enough metal in the gun to make a full-size planting spade, we added additional steel. We shaped this material—taken from Jeffrey's supply of tool-grade 4140—with

the Chambersburg, placed the gun's remains atop, added borax, and returned everything to the forge.

After we had painted the walls with slag again, I studied the blank as it cooled. A thin line was visible at the union between the gun's material and the other metal. That hairline was a reminder of how easily our plan could fail. If the two steels didn't stick together well enough, I had ruined the gun for nothing.

The line bothered Jeffrey, too. He hit the blank with a hammer, tentatively at first then hard. Nothing gave. Placing a chisel on the seam, he struck it. No fissure opened.

———

3. MARK AND PUNCH THE EYE.

A tool must have an eye, the hole its handle will be fitted into. When the blank—now a solid rectangle six-inches long, two-and-a-half-inches tall, and one-and-one-eighth-inch wide—was cool enough to touch, I measured along its top and struck two dead-center marks into the surface with a pointed scrap of hardened steel. Repeating this process on the bottom, I returned the blank to the forge.

From a rack on the wall, I retrieved the punch we had used on practice tools plus a small tin of graphite powder. Jeffrey fetched a sledgehammer and a bucket of water.

The punch had a foot-long wooden handle. One end of its steel head was a flat striking surface and the other tapered to a narrow hardened wedge. This was the cutting surface, the part we would drive through the hot blank with sledgehammer blows.

"Remember," he said. "Three hammer strikes, then cool the punch in water. Dip the tip in graphite before coming back to the blank. If the punch sticks, rock the handle until it pulls free."

I made minute adjustments, knowing that if my hand wavered or Jeffrey's initial blow was anything other than true, the punch would tilt out of plumb, skewing our cut. Many things could go wrong and most of them threatened to ruin our blank.

That's mostly not a problem in a workshop. If one piece of metal is ruined, another can be made to take its place. "Steel's cheap," I've heard blacksmiths say, but that was not how I felt about the metal I retrieved from the forge.

"*Strike!*" Jeffrey shouted. The blow rang up my arm.

"*Strike,*" he yelled, as soon as I had recentered and steadied the punch, then swung again. "Tilt it to me. Too much—back a little. *Strike!*"

I pulled the punch clear and thrust its reddened tip into the water, where it hissed, boiled, and sent up a gout of steam. Dredging the wet metal in graphite, I brought it back to the anvil and nestled its tip into the half-inch-deep channel that we had made.

By degrees, we drove straight down through the top of the blank until more than an inch of the punch was buried. The tool grew hot very quickly and became hard to remove. Once, we had to knock it free with the sledgehammer.

Flipping the blank, we drove in from the other side. Jeffrey swung for all he was worth, and I struggled to keep a firm grip on the tongs.

"Look at that," Jeffrey said, when a bit of red-hot metal finally broke free and fell clear. He took the tongs and examined the clean narrow void we had cut through the blank's center. "As straight as you can get."

4. FORGE EYE TO APPROPRIATE DIMENSIONS, BUTCHER DOWN ENDS.

When it came time for me to run the power hammer, I was nervous. It was one thing to practice with Jeffrey's inexhaustible stock of steel, another to shape my grandfather's gun. It seemed inevitable that I would make some unfixable mistake. I've seen the same thing happen with tractors and chain saws. When a novice controls a machine that magnifies force, things go wrong.

Holding the glowing blank with tongs, I walked to the hammer and set my foot against its treadle bar—a thing in function like the gas pedal of a car though not in its form. Depressing the treadle gave the tool compressed air, causing the hammerhead to fall harder and faster against the anvil. Even with the best hammers, and Jeffrey's were excellent, there is a knack to controlling the strength of the blow.

I set the hammer moving, thinning the blank's middle section. When that was done, we returned to the Chambersburg. I carried the yellow-hot blank, Jeffrey a wedge-shaped handled implement called a butcher.

I bent low beside the Chambersburg, holding the glowing metal. Jeffrey positioned the butcher above the blank. His first strike knocked the tongs from my hands.

"That happened," he said, "because you had the blank crooked on the anvil. You need to keep it straight like this"—he reached over and jostled my hands up and down—"and *this*." He twisted the tongs out of plumb from left to right. "If we go wrong either way, it'll be hard to get the rest of this right."

I took a breath, bent again, steadied my hands, and tried for dead level. Jeffrey set the wedge in place and hit it hard.

"Better," he said, striking twice more. The butcher cut deeply but left the eye intact, isolating the metal that would become the tool's shovel into an oversize glowing thumb. He measured the depth of the cut.

"Take a heat," he said. "We'll do the hoe end next."

---

5. FORGE HOE AND SHOVEL TO PRE-FROG DIMENSIONS, WELD ON ORNAMENTAL SECTIONS OF BARREL AND CYLINDER.

I worked the blank on a hammer with rounded dies, spreading material that would become the shovel's blade into a long flat tongue. When that was done, I took up the cross sections we had cut from the barrel and cylinder, and arranged them on the shovel's upper face: two sections of cylinder with a pair of barrel wafers nestled together between them. Sprinkling it all with borax, we brought the temperature up. When all was ready, I ran the white-hot metal to the Chambersburg and Jeffrey brought five hundred pounds of hammer crashing down.

After several hits, we inspected the results. The cross sections had been driven deeply into the steel. Only a thin outline defined them.

"Take a heat," Jeffrey said, looking pleased. He climbed atop his sitting anvil.

"Archaeologists used to argue about how people got started

smelting and working iron," he said. "The ore is everywhere. By weight, it makes up most of the planet."

Hammer arm aching, I listened.

"At the earth's surface, though, it's hardly ever found in workable forms except for meteoritic iron, which is rare. For a while, nobody could tell how early smiths did it. Archeologists would find iron tools but not the structures necessary to make them. That's because the earliest furnaces were disposable—clay chimneys that would last for one or two firings before breaking down.

"Now we know how they did it, but that's not the same as knowing what possessed them to develop the process. It isn't like working with copper or lead. You can't accidentally make iron in a campfire. The temperatures involved are greater than anything human beings regularly create. It's a multistep process that doesn't make sense unless you understand the chemistry, which people didn't then. Still, they were doing things like hauling tin ore from Cornwall to the Middle East. They were experimenting with furnaces and a fairly precise process that, even now, with digital thermometers and adjustable blowers, we have to work hard to get right.

"The fascinating question," he said. "Is what made people— the first ones—try so hard at what they couldn't have known was possible."

It was midafternoon by then. My palms were blistered. The thought of the ancients tinkering with ore did not surprise me. "It is entirely in our nature," I said to Jeffrey, "to mess with things that seem impossible."

He nodded at the furnace and I went to work. In contrast to the shovel, which had to be drawn out lengthwise, the hoe end needed to be fanned laterally into a fish tail. To accomplish this, I hammered outward from the centerline, working the steel between fullering dies.

"Heat," he said. "Next, we'll shape it."

Jeffrey returned to his anvil and settled in to wait. Comfortable on the work-polished surface, he passed several minutes in perfect silence.

---

6. DEFINE FROG, FORGE TO FINAL DIMENSIONS, GRIND BOTH ENDS OF THE TOOL TO SHAPE.

I had finished the delicate work of sculpting a central ridge on each of the tool's blades—the part that Jeffrey and I called the frog—and after several heats and many shouted instructions, I had returned the tool to the forge. We sat waiting for the steel to heat, Jeffrey on one anvil, I on another. We were both tired. I watched him from the corner of my eye, thinking about our chosen forms of work.

My materials had always been growing, living ones—grass, animals, wood. To me, metal was a dead medium scraped from the nonconsenting earth. It was the cold unbeating heart of modern life.

But in Jeffrey's shop, metal came alive. It writhed and spread, taking one form then another. It changed under our living hands, seemingly organically, into shapes meant for good work. It came through the door disused or rusty and left shining. This made it, I realized, not dead but deathless.

I took heat after heat, working the spade's two ends toward their finished dimensions. Sometime late that afternoon, swinging a hammer, I got thinking about the fact that every tool essential to my life as a rancher was made of steel. Every seed I've ever planted was cut into the ground by forged metal. Every nail I had driven had been beaten into shape. Blacksmithing, in its modern, industrialized form, put the roof over my head and held the walls together. I had not considered that before.

In a lull during our work, I tried conveying these thoughts to Jeffrey.

He was silent for a while, then said: "It's time."

Thinking he meant the forge, I glanced in its direction. He didn't stir from his anvil.

"It's time," he said, "for us, as a society, to technologically castrate ourselves. It has become too easy to produce new things from metal, and too easy for those objects to propagate and perpetuate themselves in our lives."

He paused, scratching with a stained, large-knuckled finger at a fleck on the anvil's surface.

"Like assault rifles," I said.

"Like a lot of things. Here, in this shop, I have the luxury of using simple tools. I build and understand them. I can fix my tools, which isn't true of most people. That's not how the larger world works. Not how necessary, practical, or complicated things are made anymore. I don't build what people *need*. Industries and corporations do that. A craftsman can't compete with their speed and economy.

"If all you wanted," he said, "was a tool that could plant trees, the factories of the world could give it to you in a minute for less than the cost of the time and materials we've used here.

"But you don't want that, which is why we're making something beautiful and useful that can't be replicated at scale—something handmade precisely for your purpose. By the end of making it, you'll understand what it's worth."

7. DRIFT THE EYE, SHAPE HOE AND SHOVEL BLADES, ADJUST ALIGNMENT AS NECESSARY.

In contrast to the rest of our labors that day, Jeffrey and I accomplished the final steps of the process entirely by hand. We used a drift—a long tapered wedge of steel—to part and spread the slit that we had punched through the blank that morning. This would give the tool its eye, the space to add the handle.

What sounds like a simple operation—one person lines up the drift, the other whacks it with the sledgehammer—wasn't. By that point in the process, the tool's hoe and shovel had become delicate. I had hammered each to its proper thinness. The shovel end was perhaps a quarter-inch thick at the tip, the hoe more fragile still.

The trick was to hit the drift hard enough to spread the eye without bending, nicking, or otherwise deforming everything else that mattered. Jeffrey had a special knee-high metal table for the task. Its legs were solid, its top a slab of two-inch-thick steel with a central hole through which the drift's tip could be hammered.

Pulling my tree spade from the forge, I brought it to where he stood ready, sledgehammer in hand. We started the split with a chisel. We followed the chisel with the drift.

"Strike!"

The hammer earned us half an inch of progress. He swung again, hitting hard, then kept at it while I held the drift in place. We worked for several heats, drifting one side of the spade then the other, spreading the eye into a long oval that tapered to a point at either end. The almond eye, Jeffrey called it.

Once, toward the end, my grip slackened enough to let the tool bounce when the hammer came down.

"Hold it tight!" Jeffrey said. "We're close. Don't fuck it up now."

Three hammer strokes later, the eye opened with a flaring symmetrical grace and only the tool's final shaping remained. I did this at the anvil, under close scrutiny, hammering the hoe and shovel across the horn until they were properly dished. Straightening the tool's axis in a vise, I sighted down its length. With a few careful blows, I gave the hoe a downward tilt to put it at the right angle for slicing grass.

I held the thing up as the metal lost its color. It was long-nosed and wide-tailed. From the top, it looked like a whale flexing its tail, preparing to sound. Segments of the barrel and cylinder remained visibly, unmistakably embossed in the shovel's upper face. I looked at those circles within circles, the tracks where bullets used to run. It had cooled beyond the working temperatures, hardening into the shape it would carry for the rest of my life. The metalwork was done.

12

THE WILD SPRING

I WOKE AT DAWN to the two-toned calling of chickadees. It was a fine, clear morning after a rain and the ground was soft. Taking my tree spade, I went out from the house through the fields. The sun had not crept above the mountains and the peaks were a dark jagged line against blue. The tool's handle, which I had finished shaping the day before, was smooth in my grasp. It was hard, close-grained wood—quite possibly our farm's only straight piece of hawthorn.

In our upper pasture, I reached the spring and looked along its length. The banks were raw, the channel bottom dark with rainwater or seepage. The year's runoff would come soon, I knew, and the water would rise.

Choosing a place a few feet from the spring, I held the spade with its hoe end downward, swung overhead, and began peeling up a three-foot square of sod. The grass was low and freshly green. The tool was satisfyingly heavy. When I brought it down hard, the sharpened edge cut even the densest roots. Sometimes the blade hit glacial cobble, rebounding with a ringing noise. I thumbed the edge after the first few impacts but soon gave it up. The stones left only small divots. It was good steel.

I cut patches for an hour or so, learning to make efficient use of the spade's heft and balance. The main danger was in striking a rock and having the blade carom into my shin. This happened midway through the morning, a glancing blow that sent me hobbling and cursing around the pasture. Thereafter, I spread my legs as I would have to swing an axe. As with splitting firewood, I felt the labor in my shoulders and back.

When the hoe cut into the ground and stuck fast, I pushed the handle away from me, levering the turf upward. It made a noise like cloth tearing, and I found that if I worked carefully I could clear the grass in long strips. Flipping these over, I arranged them along the downhill side of my excavations. The upended grass would die. The piled sod made shallow basins that would hold water. It was slow going but satisfying in the manner of peeling an orange.

At the house, I filled a wheelbarrow with seedlings. Some of them—serviceberries, aspens, cattails, wild plums—I had harvested from groves on the farm. The rest came from the state conservation nursery thirty minutes down the highway in Missoula. From them I had ponderosas, alders, dogwoods, and Douglas firs in narrow foot-tall plastic containers. I had many dozen smaller plants, too, shrubs and baby trees with bare roots or soil plugs the size and shape of popsicles. The smallest pines were packed in lots of twenty-four and cost less than two dollars apiece. This seemed a bargain for trees that grew one hundred feet tall and lasted for centuries.

At the spring, I swung the spade with all my strength, and its tip sank far into the ground. I lifted the handle, dislodging a narrow plug of earth. Swinging twice more from different angles, I made the first hole deeper and round.

I retrieved a ponderosa seedling from a bag in the wheelbarrow. It was astonishingly minute, half the diameter of a pencil, and so flexible that it drooped to one side when I held it out of plumb. That plant was almost nothing, just a brown whip with one scant corona of needles on a terminal bud. It was hard to have faith in such a thing's survival.

I knelt, holding the miniature trunk between thumb and fore-finger. With the other hand, I crumbled soil beneath and around the roots. My excavation was just six inches across, but the sapling looked like an infant put down in a king-size bed.

I gave it water, fetching gallon by gallon from the nearby spring with a long-handled dipper made from an old cook pot and a peeled limb. I mulched around the stem with three inches of wood chips.

Two hundred yards beyond the ankle-high ponderosa, I could see the mature forest at our farm's uppermost corner. Standing between me and the morning's low sun, the huge trees were so deeply green as to look almost black—a rampart of growth un-derhung with darkness. It was clear and crisp, the sky scoured by wind. The light was a piercing yellow that brought to mind higher, colder valleys I had known.

I planted with a will, setting tree after tree. I clumped silver sage in groups of two and three in drier soils, put alders and wil-lows near the water, and interspersed snowberry plants with the pines and firs. Standing among the seedlings, I felt like a man who had broken a long fast.

Off in the valley, a neighbor was plowing. I could hear the tractor engine and the scrape of steel on rock. Down there, sod was turning over, rolling off the moldboard in a slow-breaking wave.

When I hear that sound or see a plow working, I always remember the wheat fields of southeast Washington. The Palouse, as that corner of the state is prettily called, is the breadbasket and wine cellar of the Pacific Northwest. Its earth is a rich, deep loess, a largesse of Pleistocene flooding that has been wind-sculpted into a dryland farmer's paradise. It is a rare, valuable soil from which fortunes are made in grain.

Having lived there as a college student, always marveling at the earth's curvaceous fertility, I know that the Palouse is beautiful. It is a landscape of belly, breast, and shoulder—a place that a young person feels in the pit of the stomach. Beneath this beauty lies a sense of loss and callous misuse—a tinge of absence and obscenity as faint as the scent of turned earth but abundant. When I see those wheat fields, I cannot help noticing that something enormous has been broken.

That is the case in January when everything is under snow in the Palouse, in June when the crops are ripening, and in September when the stalks are shorn, but the effect is never so pronounced as in springtime when half of the fields are plowed and the rest come up in winter wheat. Nothing is quite like early springtime in the Palouse. Nearly every square foot of ground is planted or shortly will be. The effect is gorgeous and harsh. The land's simultaneous fecundity and emptiness, its raw readiness for seed, is so evident as to bring actual pain into a heart.

A year before I started to plant saplings on our farm in the Jocko Valley, I drove through eastern Washington at precisely that heart-aching season. I turned from the two-lane highway outside Washtucna onto a side road indistinguishable from a dozen others except for the fact that it cut through a basalt ravine beside a small stream. Changing into shorts, I left the car and ran along the road.

The wash had proved too steep to plow. Wild rye grew in bunches, last year's dry stalks rising chest-high. I saw bluebunch wheatgrass, fescue, and rabbitbrush—plants common to the native rangelands of Montana. I recognized the prairie.

A hawk coasted over and ground squirrels scattered. Songbirds flushed from a thin line of willows. For a few hundred yards, I ran across the warp and weft of nature's whole cloth. Such places are rare in the Palouse.

Leaving the gully, the road climbed a long gradual hill toward a homestead. The house was small, with a commanding view of sprouts and fallow. A tall gabled barn stood beside it, flanked by rows of shelterbelt trees and skewing patrician with its ornate cupola and wrought-iron wind vane. It was a fine, solitary spot, the kind of site I might have chosen for a farm.

Because of the sun's direction, the trees and buildings were cutout shapes. It was only as I came to the hilltop that I saw how the plank siding had split and shattered, and that the house's front door hung askew. I stopped in the road and crows flew from the hayloft's broken windows. A windmill stood in the yard facing the southwest wind with half its blades missing. It did not turn.

A lifetime of energy and effort had been lavished on that homestead. The place had been everything to someone, a realm. When the windcharger spun and hummed, farmers would have sat evenings in the warm glow of homegrown light, feeling secure on the land, believing that they would remain. They were wrong. They were gone. That is the terror and promise of an abandoned farm.

I could hear a diesel engine. Its source—a behemoth rubber-tracked tractor pulling forty feet of disc plow—hove shortly into view. Emerging from a fold in the hills, the machine crossed a low plain. It moved smoothly, inexorably, its implement darkening the ground in passing. When it was nearest to me, a quarter mile off, I raised a hand to the operator though I could not see him in the cab.

I ran for miles. The first abandoned homestead disappeared behind me and another—similarly empty and weather-checked—appeared. The road cut straight past. One side of the right-of-way was coming up in wheat seedlings. The other was corduroyed bare dirt as far as I could see.

Every few hundred yards, a heap of translucent herbicide jugs filled the ditch. Empties. I stopped and read the labels, recognizing a proprietary brew that killed everything except a single strain of wheat that had been genetically modified to resist it. The chemical seemed to be keeping its promises. Nothing else grew.

Nothing, that is, until I followed the road onto a low flat and found a single six-inch-high yarrow plant rooted where packed gravel met and mixed with soil. It was a pale-green sprout with pennant leaves jutting from a single stalk. I got to my knees and looked at it, smelled it. One wild trespasser in the kingdom of wheat.

A spray rig was working the hills north of the road, appearing now on a green crest then in a trough, trailing mist from a boom nearly the width of a football field. Farther ahead and with a sudden roar, a crop duster cut into view above the horizon, heeled over like a stricken warplane, and vanished. It made a series of dives, closer with each pass. I wondered if the pilot could see me or the sprig at my feet.

Herbicide began to taint the wind, making it hard to draw a proper breath. I ran back along the road as fast as I could go.

There was a time when I thought planting was planting whether a person did it by hand or with a six-hundred-horsepower tractor, whether pine trees or wheat seed went into the ground. Standing beside the spring, newly forged spade in hand and my neighbor's tractor fading in and out behind the constant sound of water, things looked differently.

In the endless cultivated fields of the Palouse and elsewhere, I've seen countless abandoned houses, men and women grafted to gargantuan machines, a crop duster strafing soil. I've seen chemical containers heaped by the hundreds, each one knifed open by someone in such a hurry that he or she could not wait while two-and-a-half gallons of liquid poured through the mouth of a jug.

From this mad rush to keep the wheels turning, we reap a uniquely modern blend of desperation and loneliness. The loneliness follows from erasing a complex ecology and forcing a single crop on tired soil. Desperation is what we're left with once the West is won.

FOR THE FIRST FEW days of planting seedlings near the little stream on our farm, I was particular about which species went where and in what quantities. After that, I used whatever I could transplant or afford so long as it was native to the region or particularly useful to wildlife. I scribbled notes in the margins of my journal: "12 Currant—8 Ash—48 Douglas Fir—3 Narrowleaf Cattails—24 Sandbar Willow," but I quickly lost track of what was what. The work became a pleasing, grimy blur. I labored until the plants were gone, scraped more sod, went to the nursery, began anew.

Gillian helped. Her hands, like mine, learned the shapes of seedlings and their roots. Pine was straight, taproot to leader. Dogwood was thin and fine, its branches too easily broken. Snowberry was a knot of vigorous potential. Sage was rigid, with mirror-image menorahs of branch and root.

When I watched her pack dirt around a fragile stem, I liked thinking of the forest that might grow. Some of the trees would die, I knew. But some could become behemoths. It entered my head that our children, if we had any, might stand under their branches.

After that, it became hard to plant imperfectly. I dug better holes and abandoned ones that seemed unsuitable. I thought on a longer timeframe, arranging plants so they would not shade each other for decades. I took more care with the roots.

By late May, my palms and the spade's hawthorn handle had polished each other to a hard sheen. My back had accepted the job's particular strain. One afternoon, I stood up and shook the dirt from an empty pot. I looked for the next seedling and could find none. The first year's planting was through.

That night or the next, deer came through like a horde of vandals. They topped chokecherries, defoliated every alder and dogwood, and reduced the willows to bare whips. The destruction was complete enough to stun me. I had expected damage but not on that scale or so quickly.

I spent two days driving off the herd in the mornings and evenings before giving it up as futile. They ran from me but tiptoed back. I protected what I could, making cages around the larger plants with old steel fence posts and wire. I could not save everything, but the cages worked well enough to keep me hopeful until midsummer. Then the rodents developed a hunger for cambium.

A vole is an innocent-looking thing—a fat short-tailed mouse that does not run but trundles unhurriedly through the grass on short legs. They are not clever, but they must be good breeders to exist on this farm, as they do, at a density not less than one per square foot of pasture. When snowmelt bares the ground in spring, every field is crisscrossed with their meandering tunnels and grooves.

Unreasonably temerarious, voles often stand their ground when pursued. If a dog gives chase, they come to bay like miniature bears, squealing and leaping at their giant antagonist's face. I have seen one bite down hard on the toe of Gillian's boot and hang there by its teeth.

In August, the dim little stalwarts came for the trees. I went out one day with my dipping bucket and noticed that several ponderosas had yellowed. I watered the plants heavily but returned two days later to find them worse. Down on my hands and knees, I found a narrow ring of chewed cambium an inch or two from the ground. The damage was easily overlooked but fatal. The voles always ate a complete circle around the tiny trunks. A girdled tree is dead before the branches wilt.

I crawled all over the planting, looking at the gnawed bases of willows, sage, and pine. The voles had no preferences when it came to species. They liked everything we'd planted. Where they found phloem, they feasted.

If ranching has taught me anything, though, it's how to put my head down and work. Buying rolls of small-gauge construction mesh, I made cylinders to protect the base of each seedling. The voles kept pace, climbing over, under, and through. Everywhere I looked were withering girdled stems.

At times, I was certain that the voles would leave nothing alive. Once or twice in late August, I stood at the center of my planting, surveyed the destruction, and indited myself for the sin—a mortal one in America—of wasting time and money.

As summer turned to fall that year, I learned how plants die by stages—from the top down if eaten by deer or parched by heat, from the bottom up if voles have gnawed the bark to ribbons. I grew skilled at noticing subtle foreshocks: a green turned powdery, the strength gone from a toothpick-gauge branch.

Even as the damage mounted, I kept faith in the tool that Jeffrey and I had crafted. A season's digging had scoured its cutting edges clean. I oiled the steel after every use, taking better care of the tree spade than I had of my grandfather's Smith & Wesson. Kept up that way, it would last a lifetime. No matter what happened to my first year's planting, I could continue the work.

That fall, I hunted with two friends in the sage and mountain country south of Dillon, Montana. We ranged through steep terrain in a frigid wind, living with our parka hoods up for days. Usually that landscape crawls with hunters, but on that trip, we seemed to be the only people in the high country. Nobody else had been foolish enough to go out. While we were hunkered on the crest of a particularly exposed ridge, examining the frozen world through binoculars, a gust threw one of my companions head over heels downhill.

The sky was cloudless. At night, the stars looked clear and low enough to pick like fruit. Dense, dry snowdrifts lay in the lee of every tree and bush, but otherwise the ground was scoured bare.

Finding elk on the fourth afternoon, we climbed straight up for two hours and I killed a large cow in talus so steep that I wondered how she stood upright on it. I had no doubts as I crept to a boulder and set my rifle across it. I felt no tremors. My breath came easily, though I was conscious of the wind and penetrating cold. When I fired, she dropped senseless while the rest of the herd sheeted away like spilled water off a table. I clambered toward her, expecting the remorse that had always come with taking the lives of animals.

As I picked my way in her direction, a different feeling entered me. I was aware of what I had done and sorry that the cow would not see spring, but I felt no shame or guilt. She had been one animal among a hundred and the herd would persevere. The wild country would shelter, feed, and increase them. Gillian and I would eat well through winter.

Reaching the cow, I found that I could stand near death and remain at peace. Concerning the work to come—evisceration, hauling meat out of the mountains—I felt only a deep sense of gratitude. I was certain that I had been given a gift and wondered how to respond in kind. I thought that perhaps I should plant more trees so deer and elk could shelter in them. Perhaps I should come back here in the spring to pull invasive weeds along the trail. Perhaps, on the farm, I might find a way to feed other people as well as the mountains were feeding me. I was happy thinking along such lines. I felt fine, calm, and at home.

13

SHADE

IN MID-MARCH OF THE second year of planting, I pulled back the dead grass that the snowdrifts had pressed around the stem of a year-old dogwood. The plant had entered winter in good shape. My hopes were high.

An inch off the soil, though, I found a familiar ring of ragged wood. Above it, the stem was brittle. Snapping the dead stick, I tossed the broken piece away. It was a small loss, but my worries multiplied as I walked along the spring. In several places, I couldn't find a seedling that looked to have survived.

For several weeks, I was convinced that I had thrown away my prior spring and summer. A few plants—mostly conifers—were unscathed. The rest seemed lifeless.

In April, I passed the same dead dogwood and stooped to pull up the remainder of its stem. The roots did not yield. I tugged harder with both hands. Something in the way it resisted made me look closer.

Hardly visible above the soil, a delicate shoot had daylighted. Though tiny, it stood out vividly against the winterkilled thatch.

Within days, the same contrast was visible across the planting. Gnawed trees, particularly the deciduous, water-loving ones, suckered up from their roots. The stumps of deer-browsed shrubs broke bud.

Such unexpected survival encouraged me. Fencing the cattle out of a piece of the adjacent pasture, I began to double the planting's size, making it nearly two acres. This time, I protected each seedling with a foot-high cylinder of narrow-gauge metal mesh.

It was a beautiful springtime. Up and down the little watercourse, trees and shrubs rose from the dead. The weather was comfortably, unseasonably warm. I dug and planted in a T-shirt and shorts when in other years I'd have expected late, wet snows. The plants looked happy. They reached for the sun, leaves unfolding against an unremittingly blue sky.

The sky was like that throughout May and nobody in the valley complained. It was only after we all baled hay two weeks early without a single cloudburst that neighbors mentioned the lack of rain.

We ought not have been surprised. From the start, the year was destined to be a rough one. The snowpack was thin and March stayed dry enough to set local records. Summer's true and unforgiving character, however, did not show itself until mid-June when the heat arrived. The temperature began rising shortly after I had finished planting and it built in strength over a week. Monday was a normal seventy-degree early-summer day. By Friday, we were living in a furnace.

The whole West was. In Seattle, my parents were sweating through hundred-degree afternoons. Portland, Oregon, had an unprecedented 116 degrees Fahrenheit for three days in a row.

What the news called a "heat dome" sat on the Jocko Valley like a broody hen. For a month, there was nothing but clear sky, a burning sun, and the hot steady wind drinking moisture from the ground. Cattle huddled in the meager shade of hawthorn trees. Where no roots held it and no grass blocked the sun, the earth became powder.

The mountains, which I have cherished every day since moving here, vanished behind a gray-blue drop cloth. To be smoked out by forest fires is nothing new in Montana, but to have the smoke arrive before the Fourth of July and stay all summer is remarkable. That year, it came mostly from enormous distant conflagrations. One in Oregon—straight up the prevailing wind—burned four hundred thousand acres and sent its haze as far as Vermont. Half-a-dozen smaller blazes pocked the mountains between our farm and the Idaho line.

Ash in the air and on windows made it seem as if the world might never get clean. Every evening, the sun turned bloodred at eight o'clock while it was still well above the western mountains. It looked alien and unwell. I stared without shading my eyes.

The new seedlings endured these conditions hardily for a while. Planting had given them a blush of growth. For several weeks, I could sit among plucky, hopeful sprigs and pretend that the summer wasn't doing a passable impression of an apocalypse. By the end of June, though, leaves began to wilt and blanch.

From then on, I spent my spare hours watering. In the planting's first year, I had relied on the spring's flow and a long-handled dipper. The thing worked well, but the work grew difficult as the number of saplings ran into the hundreds and my forest-to-be extended farther from the creek. Each plant took three scoops of water. Every dipper load meant a fifty-yard walk.

In the second year, I connected a long plastic pipe to the farm's pressurized stock-water line. This allowed me to stand in the ever-present smoke and heat, snake a hose among vole tubes and deer cages, and water six hundred seedlings. The job took most of a day, and with the many other tasks of running a farm during a drought, I found it hard to keep up. Signs of stress—drooping stems and yellow-tinged leaves—were everywhere.

I felt similarly blanched. I was short-tempered and strangely tired that summer. Every morning, I woke up feeling weak. In the evenings, I drank glass after glass of water but could not slake my thirst.

By late July, parched grass crumbled underfoot. Where our flood-irrigation water could not reach, the ground was iron-hard and pale. Because it was too hot to keep our farmhouse windows shut, Gillian and I lived with stinging eyes and parched throats. We woke up mornings with ash in our mouths.

One night at the height of the heat, she came into the living room and told me that we would have a child. We were tired from a day's work, our skins patterned with sweat and dust. Her eyes were very wide as she crossed the linoleum floor. I leaned against the kitchen counter, holding her. Joy and many other fine feelings came into our hearts but also fear.

Encountering that fear among our hopes was like finding a rattlesnake in the garden. At first, I supposed it came from knowing the risks of pregnancy and worrying that Gillian might get hurt. Then there was the fact that when the baby arrived true rest would become a stranger in our house.

That was part of the fear but not its entirety. It was only weeks later, watering seedlings in the smoke, that I understood the root: I was scared by the viciousness of that summer.

July was the warmest month in recorded history, globally and in our region. Week by week, record books got rewritten. Reservoirs were depleted to unheard-of levels before August and I kept hearing stories about cattlemen selling off prized herds. Looking at the vast sky I had loved since childhood, I found it low-ceilinged and unrecognizable.

Clouds were supposed to bear up from the west, dark and heavy with rain. That always happened when the hay lay vulnerable in windrows. The clouds did not come. After several weeks, it became impossible to ignore the fact that something essential had faltered. Even people who refused to say the words "climate change" could feel what was in the air. I'm certain of that. All but the dullest of them knew.

Into this world—a crowded, baking planet; a culture apparently bent on ecocide; a national history of violence; a rampant pandemic; an uncertain future—we proposed to bring a child. Gillian and I worked all day, every day, in our gray horizonless valley. We slept under a starless sky. It seemed a fearful place to raise our daughter or son.

Around that time, I was building fence on a neighbor's place when a storm came in. From the hilltop where I was working, I watched leaden, scalloped clouds slide in to cap the valley's gridded fields. The wind was violent, raising dust from all the gravel roads. I watched the clouds hungrily, hopefully. I told myself that they would crack like eggs and spill the rain.

Two fields away, someone cutting a thin crop of hay stopped his tractor and ran for cover, leaving the machine. The wind chased him home, scattering his neat, concentric rows. A wheel-line sprinkler sat in another pasture, its spray lifting off at an angle and vanishing. No water reached the ground. The dry air took it all.

Beyond the running farmer, a bright thread licked down. Its ghost was still in my eyes when the thunder came. Out toward our farm. I saw a second strike, then another in the foothills. There was no moisture in that storm, only dry lightning to blast the fields and peaks. Sheltering in a dell, I checked the weather on my phone and found ten more days of sun and wind predicted, another week at ninety-five degrees.

The plume, when it came, surprised no one. When I first saw it rise from Jocko Canyon, a few miles east of the farm, I experienced something like a sense of relief. Having expected fire for days, I was glad to know where it was.

The wind turned. For weeks it had blown from the southwest, as it often does here, at an angle that would have pushed the blaze farther back into the mountains. That afternoon, though, the weather spun on its heel and poured from the east with a seething force.

It was a prairie wind, capable of driving fire across several timbered ridges in the course of an afternoon. Standing at our door, I felt that hot air against my chest. If it kept up long and hard enough, I knew the flames would reach our fields.

Except for the column of smoke purling westward at an angle, the air became perfectly clear. For the first time in a month, I could discern individual trees on the eastern skyline. Trees that would soon be gone.

I pulled on running shoes and trotted up the county road. Gaining the bank of an earthen irrigation canal, I followed the water through my backyard forest, thinking: *This is where I saw a sow with tiny cubs; here four badgers swam the ditch in a line; here the dog met a lion in the wayside brush; here is the broken-crowned alder where an owl sleeps; here is the ouzel pool; here, covered with small copper-winged butterflies, is the bush with the sweetest currants.*

Knowing everything might be ash and cinders within days, I ran with a conscious sense of leave-taking. It was heart-wrenching to move that way through a place I considered permanent and timeless, distressing to look at close thickets and fine shady groves knowing that they could vanish. Each insect in the air, the squirrels scolding from branches, and everything green seemed precious. I knew how small each plant had been at its sprouting, that every old-growth ponderosa had been no more than half of a vole's breakfast. The chokecherries were coming on. That they should char before ripening seemed a shame.

I circled down through the woods and over a barbwire gate, and jogged into a corner of our uppermost pasture. When I came into the open, every raptor in the valley was aloft and circling. Half-a-dozen redtails spun above me, loosely grouped and rising on the wind. Farther off were other spiraling birds.

The hawks rode upward in a sky immaculately blue except for the fire's pillar, calling with terrible clarity. A feeling like that piercing sound was everywhere that day. It entered our hearts as a nervous, urgent energy until the whole valley felt like a horse gathering itself to buck.

After dark, driving home from an errand in Arlee, I stopped to watch the fire glowing behind the ridge it was climbing. A tongue of flame went up, a skyline tree flaring brightly and quickly, like a match.

The following day, I watered. The wind was gone, but the fire was still creeping outward in every direction. Smoke pooled in the valley as the midday sun cooked down. The larches, pines, currants, and spruces—everything I had planted and protected— had a wilted look.

If each tree got a minute under the hose, the job took eight hours. Sometimes I would count off seconds. Sometimes I would stand thinking about our child who was coming, a raw awareness of new life's fragility in my mind. I wondered how a parent could protect an infant from three months of smoke or a heat that would only increase in years to come. It was one of those still, close, damnably hot days when everything rattles.

Setting the nozzle at the base of a snowberry, I headed for what I called the big alder, a title only accurate in relative terms. That sapling, one of a few from the prior year that had been overlooked by both deer and voles, had grown prodigiously. Its leader reached higher than my head. There were several healthy branches. Of everything along the spring, the big alder looked most like a proper tree.

I lay on my back in the dappled shade, which at that hour barely covered me. The trunk was broomstick-thick at ground level, its bark a freckled brown. In all my rounds with the hose, I could not remember watering that alder. I had not bothered because the tree thrived on its own. It looked green and strong whenever I passed, so I let it be.

I turned onto my stomach and probed the grass with my fingers. Where the tree's shadow fell, the ground, if not cool to the touch, wasn't hot. A hint of give remained in the soil.

Rousing, I walked off, shifted the hose to a new seedling, and returned to the alder tree. Ants filed along the trunk. Farther off in the grass, I could see the picked-clean bones of a fawn's leg— proof that coyotes came at night.

Earlier that morning, I had startled a yearling black bear from the brush beside an irrigation ditch. The animal had run scared, fleeing the valley like people abandon dense timber at dusk. It had loped toward the thigh-high grass and young trees of the spring. Halting there, it seemed to be considering whether it could take shelter. After a second, the animal ran on. *Still*, I told myself, *it paused.*

That bear was not alone in recognizing the planting as distinct from the surrounding fields. All season, animals had acted that way. Caught in open pastures, coyotes and foxes bent their lines of flight toward and through the spring. A badger returned often enough to create a minefield of holes.

A heron came to stalk the smooth dark frogs that had taken up residence on the spring's ungrazed banks. I found water snakes, killdeer, and mountain bluebirds. For an unbroken week of days, I looked out the front window each morning to see a kestrel perched on the fence brace overlooking the spring. It left the skins and spines of rodents on the uppermost barbed wire.

Anything that ate voles was a friend, but that bird was particularly familiar. A year before, I had walked past an old half-collapsed chicken coop downhill from our house to find that a small falcon had flown in through a hole in the metal mesh. When I came near, it threw itself against the chicken wire. I left the door wide open, thinking the bird would find its own way out.

The day was warm, though. Worried, I returned after a couple hours to find the kestrel weaker, clinging high in a corner, feathers ragged from struggling. I plucked it from the mesh, pinning the wings. I had worn work gloves against its talons, but the bird only watched with black eyes and panted hard between my hands. It felt like I was carrying a pounding heart.

Clear of the coop, the kestrel spread and lifted into the air as I opened my fingers. Afterward, I could recognize the bird's frayed tail. It stayed around the farm, roosting in cottonwoods.

Now the kestrel ate the rodents that had gnawed and survived on my trees. That my work fed such a hunter made me look differently at voles. Before this, I had classified the little beasts as nuisances and nemeses. I thought that they worked against me, always undoing progress.

Sitting beside the alder, I understood that voles and deer had been the first wild animals to notice my planting, the vanguard of a hoped-for older world. They were living, gnawing, troublesome proof that a change had begun.

WHEN GERMAINE AND I first discussed my grandfather's gun, she had said: "The last two hundred years were bad in the American West. It's on us to make sure that the next two hundred are better."

For months after the conversation, I held that idea in my head. Her formulation of the task was as clear, direct, and accurate as any I've encountered. I appreciated her use of the word *us*. It was confounding, though, to wake up with phrases like "two hundred years" and "American West" in mind and wonder what, really, should be done with the hours between breakfast and dinner.

When I considered the ecological and cultural desecration of a continent, the problem's scale seemed to dwarf anything I could do. I also worried that a descendent of Pilgrims and homesteaders might be damned to degrade the American continent simply by living on it no matter what he intended or attempted. Looking at the past, it was hard to believe otherwise. Briefly but seriously, I considered returning to where my people had come from— France or England—but knew that I would be foreign there.

For years, I felt the grip of a paralyzing bind: The gorgeous, pillaged West was my only home, but I saw myself and the landscape mostly through the dark lens of inherited guilt. Living this way did not draw the best from me or do much for the places I loved.

I used to keep my grandfather's gun close. In solitary moments, I held the weapon and listened as if a secret of pride, clan, and manhood might whisper from its round black mouth.

I hear a different secret now: We pick and choose our lineage.

We have agency in what we leave behind and carry on. There are certain things I love about what ranching teaches, certain qualities in the Western heart that I will not give up. A particular form of tenacity, for example—that willingness to weather storms and undertake enormously difficult work. I came out here because I loved those traits—or versions of them that became myth. I still aspire to some of those things, only now I refuse to accept them part and parcel with violence, with the worst of the past.

I think it possible to keep the best aspects of a Western heart—qualities like gumption, grit, and feral joy—without embracing the brutality that runs rampant in our history. Thoughtful people can and must separate such things. They can hunt and raise livestock while despising violence. They can farm crops and plant wild trees with the same strong hands. Sometimes, when I am watering a sprout, I invoke those people, that future, so vividly that the dream of them becomes quite nearly faith. It is the only faith I know.

The planting is small, mattering principally to me, some bears and deer, the local birds, and an empire of voles. It's dwarfed by what the Confederated Salish and Kootenai Tribes have done to restore the Jocko River. It's minuscule in comparison to the West's crying need.

Our property is a flyspeck on the map of western Montana. But as the seedlings have rooted, I have started to see it as consequential. The farm is becoming a shared space. Gillian and I still practice agriculture there. We grow raspberries and raise grass-fed cattle. We have fewer cows than the rancher who ran things before us and graze them carefully so the soil does not suffer. We sell meat locally, donating what we can to people who might otherwise go without. While we go about that labor, the saplings strain upward. Songbirds pass over them, sweeping along like leaves in a fast stream. Badgers till the soil and coyotes descend from the foothills to carouse in the twilight. We do not begrudge them a place at this table.

If I sometimes develop delusions of grandeur, they do not last. One afternoon, I lifted the tree spade overhead and thought of how I might look from a distance, silhouetted against far-off timber. *Picturesque*, I thought, *perhaps even heroic*. On the next downstroke, the tool bounced off a stone and split my shin.

The planting has done nothing to address most of what is broken in the world. I set seedlings in the ground while a neighboring field was divided into ten-acre ranchettes. I mulched at dusk while taillights burned toward a meth house up the gravel road. Hauling water against the drought, I made no progress toward equity in American society. What I do beside the spring is good work all the same. It's one of many possible beginnings of the better centuries to come.

IN MID-SEPTEMBER, A COLD strong rain came down. For a day and a night, it hammered our roof and sheeted from the eaves. Afterward, Gillian and I went walking. It had been a month or more since she had been far into the forest, the first trimester of pregnancy being what it is. A full season had passed since either of us had breathed easily outdoors.

To hike in the mountains with her is a pleasure. She has a long, easy stride and moves so well along trails that I sometimes have to stretch to keep pace. That afternoon, she covered country, walking out from our farm into the timber, from the valley toward the heights.

Things had changed since she had last been through. A thirty-yard-wide fire line had been hacked from the forest and the rutted two-track road scraped flat to accommodate equipment. The blaze had not, in the end, come.

When we climbed steeper hills, she cupped a hand between her waistband and a belly that had just begun to swell. She felt well, she said, but it was strange to carry another person everywhere. It was the first time I had looked at things that way. The child remained unborn, but we had done the trick of making three from two.

We covered miles on an old logging road that loops into Jocko Canyon through a forest drinking its fill for the first time in months. Relief was everywhere around us. Across the ridge, the fire only smoldered. New snow blanched the highest peaks.

Turning homeward, we reached the last thicket above our farm and passed two black bears on their haunches looking back. Two hundred yards on, we crossed into the planting. The turned earth was black with rain. Water hung on every leaf and stem, shining.

One night at our kitchen table, my parents described the time be-fore I entered the world. They recalled the last weeks of pregnancy, the feeling of something immense and unstoppable reaching its dramatic conclusion. My mother said: "All of a sudden, I realized that what I thought of as the end was actually the beginning."

Ever since, I've been thinking about you. You. The word is a drumbeat and a heartbeat for me now. While Gillian, your mother, creates you day by day, I have been watering small wild plants and considering the time and place you will enter. If all goes well, you will be born as I was, following the darkest part of winter. You will first glimpse life as everything breaks bud.

Perhaps this means that you, like me, will have spring's green up woven through the depths of your mind. I would be pleased to see you inherit such hope, to believe that the world should improve and flower as time goes along. It is the truth even if things go otherwise.

If we raise you as we mean to, you may well grow up loving this farm, the valley, and the hard-used, enduring, montane West. You'll live according to its seasons. It will feed you and be a true home. But one day, as you grow into your mind, you will notice that history infects the present. In your pale inner wrist, the blue blood visible under your skin, you'll mark an in-heritance you never sought. You'll face the knowledge that some of your ancestors, present since the start of North America's European colonization, have been party to episodes of cruelty and destruction so fantastic as to mock the ways in which those long-dead forebears might have been wise, kind, or gracious.

If this unsettles you, it is because your heart is good and your mind sharp. Unsettled is a fine, strong word. It can carry you beyond guilt into the realm of action.

I'm sure of very little where the future is concerned. I do not know, for example, whether we—here in the West and elsewhere—will stay thralls of cultural and ecological violence or turn unexpectedly toward justice and repair.

I offer no predictions but want to tell you something before we are in the world together, before I become your father with many flaws: I was born with hope and have it still. Even as the mountains burn. I had it even when my grandfather's gun was heaviest in my hand.

History is an hourglass tapering to us—to you. The past must come through us to reach the future. Because of this, what we embrace will endure. What we resist will begin to fade slowly from being. Since I remade the revolver, I've been convinced that you and I, alive, occupy a position of immense responsibility and creative power. There is hope in a hammer swing, though the past is stubborn metal.

On the farm, as faster-growing trees rise beyond the height of a human eye, the planting will hide its heart from view. It will fill with life. Every morning this time of year, three whitetail bucks rise from the tallest grass at sunrise and feed on what I've planted. Most days, I shout them off with instructions to wait a *year. Sometimes, though, I let the creatures browse. In a decade, those deer will be hidden, no concern of mine at all.*

The spade I made will be yours someday. But the grove—this small forest growing daily more complex and whole—belongs no more to you than to me or to the deer that come at night. You can enter, of course. I made a sitting place, hauled two boulders in and left them flat side up. You can visit always.

Come in the flush of spring or in midwinter when ponderosa bark and leafless dogwoods glow orange and red against deep snow. At the end of summer, come after a long-awaited storm to feel the great loosening peace of a thousand trees drinking. Stand in the grass while rain soaks down to the roots that hold us here.

Ever since I grew to see the American West clearly, I have been wracked by the fact that each generation since the coming of my ancestors left the place worse off—more ecologically fragmented, less just—than they found it. It struck me as wrong, this relentless tearing at the fabric of home.

I want your story to diverge from that past. It already has a different start. You will be born on a farm that holds more wild life with each passing year. You will be raised knowing, from the enduring example of the Salish and other Native tribes, that human beings can live thousands of years in a place without ruining it.

Your children, if you have any, will play among many-trunked alders and pines so thick that outspread arms cannot encircle them. You can show them arched black openings in the brush and tell them how the bears use hidden trails.

You can rest together, sheltered from the sun. They will like that, I think. In the world that is coming, they will need shade.

Acknowledgments

My infant daughter, Thea, for occasionally sleeping through the night and in no way whatsoever complicating the process of finishing a book. My wife, Gillian, for sustaining Thea, our farm, and everything else, and for agreeing to spend most of my advance on saplings. My parents, Richard Andrews and Colleen Chartier, for unfaltering encouragement and many hours spent watering the aforementioned saplings in a pitiless sun. My grandfather Robert Andrews for giving me the revolver. Gillian and Colleen again, specifically for traveling to Bigfork to photograph the process of forging.

Jeffrey Funk for opening the New Agrarian School to me and being immensely generous with time and expertise. Betsey Funk for making me feel at home every time I came to work. Germaine White for excellent black currant jam and conversation. Dan'l Moore for starting my blacksmithing education.

Michael Hicks and Nathaniel Ian Miller for their close reading of drafts and complete unwillingness to please. David James Duncan for being kind enough to place my work in lofty company.

Naomi Gibbs for seeing merit in this project. Ivy Givens for her keen editorial eye and patience while discussing issues large and small. Duvall Osteen for wheeling, dealing, and handing down stylish baby clothes. David Hough for the very best kind of pointy-headed nitpicking. Everyone who contributed to this project at HarperCollins—Laura Brady, Pam Barricklow, Brian Moore, Kerry Rubenstein, Chloe Foster, Tavia Kowalchuk, Taylor Turkington, and Kelly Cronin—for sharing in the mountain of work that stands between a good story and a finished book.